Endangered Spouses

The Legacy of Marital Inequality

Lenora Greenbaum Ucko

University Press of Am
Lanham • New York • 1

D0814376

Copyright © 1995 by
University Press of America,® Inc.
4720 Boston Way
Lanham, Maryland 20706

3 Henrietta Street
London, WC2E 8LU England

Library of Congress Cataloging-in-Publication Data

Ucko, Lenora Greenbaum.
Endangered spouses : the legacy of marital inequality / Lenora Greenbaum
Ucko.
p.   cm.
Includes bibliographical references and index.
1. Marriage.   2. Marriage--Folklore.   3. Tales.
I. Title.
HQ728.U35   1995
306.81--dc20   94-40686 CIP

ISBN 0-8191-9807-2 (cloth: alk paper)
ISBN 0-8191-9808-0 (pbk: alk paper)

To my father
Louis Sverdlik
who taught me
to love the stories

Contents

Acknowledgements

I owe professional debts of gratitude to many people. To all who read earlier sections of the book, who discussed various ideas about form and content with me, and who made suggestions about publication, I extend my deep appreciation. I would like to give special recognition to some who made distinctive contributions to this work.

Foremost is Amy Grant, a scholar in English and American literature, who contributed in many ways. From a feminist perspective, she repeatedly evaluated my ideological statements. As a writer, she suggested stylistic improvements. From her editorial knowledge, she corrected editorial errors. As a friend, she gave moral support and helped me overcome the usual bouts of despair that accompany a work in progress. I thank her for it all.

Helen Hacker is a scholar in women's studies and family relations and a long-time colleague and friend. Her keen judgment and helpful ideas were precise, relevant and very welcome. Though a frank and sometimes blunt critic, she tempers her comments with collegial respect and personal affection, which I greatly appreciate.

Beverly Stoeltje of the Folklore Institute of Indiana University read earlier portions of this work, offered valuable suggestions, and strongly encouraged its completion. W.F.H. Nicolaisen, Professor Emeritus at SUNY-Binghamton, has consistently supported my use of folklore in diverse scholarly projects, including this one.

Sandra Eisdorfer, formerly at the University of North Carolina Press at Chapel Hill, offered suggestions about manuscript preparation and friendly support when both were very much needed. She has my gratitude. Johannah Sherrer, the former director of the Reference

Department at Duke University's Perkins Library, made life much easier by her relentless efforts and her special skill to find whatever elusive source I needed. I am grateful for her help.

To the students in my classes at Adelphi University, Duke University, Durham Technical Community College, and Fort Bragg School for International Studies, I owe many thanks for listening, discussing, arguing, and helping me to clarify the different aspects of marriage in and out of folkstories. To them and to all the others who were helpful along the way, my special thanks.

My husband, Henry Zvi Ucko, deserves a prominent place among the long-suffering spouses of the writers of books. As a writer himself, he was unstinting in his readiness to read and reread the manuscript for both style and content. His discerning eye and rigorous logic were invaluable assets. He helped with the proofreading and much of the editing prior to publication. And as a husband, he found himself drawn into many spirited discussions about marriage. For all these efforts, he has a grateful wife.

The challenge of explaining modern marriage to my children, when they were growing up, and to students in my classes, led to a deeper inquiry and to writing this book. My hope is for happy marriages for them all.

L.G.U.
Durham, NC

1
Out of the Past: A Beginning

Marriage has long presented a perplexing paradox. Eagerly embraced as the basis of a good life, marriage is nevertheless a source of disappointment and disillusionment for many spouses. We tend to explain a particular couple's unhappiness in terms of unique personal failings and incompatibilities. Marriage failures in general are blamed on new social trends, such as changes in occupation and life style, and the prevalence of cultural ideologies of permissiveness and personal freedom. Overlooked in these analyses is an age-old legacy perpetuating an environment of marital strife. This book addresses that heritage.

Described in the *Book of Proverbs* as worth more than rubies and as a crown to her husband, the wife is considered a great good. Men are urged to marry because without a wife, there is no help, joy, blessing, or atonement. Another description of women is quite different. When seen as contentious or wicked, woman is a scourge worse than death, unwanted even by the devil, and more dangerous than lions and dragons. This double view continues to the present in myth, the media, and popular parlance.

Despite their popularity, these views are distortions of reality. Certainly less than perfect, women like men are not all good or all bad. Research is finding more and more evidence that except for the most obvious physical and reproductive differences, women and men are essentially the same kind of beings.[1] In a world where physical prowess is no longer critical for economic success, women are proving to be the equal of men in many fields of endeavor, for example, law, medicine, computer programming. Even in areas long considered a male preserve, such as the military, women are proving to be equal contributors.

In spite of these findings, the issue of gender equality remains a problem in today's world. Society still places the major responsibility on wives for child rearing, domestic chores, catering to a husband, and generally maintaining good family relations. Many women feel this to be clearly a heavy and unwarranted burden. Furthermore, women are often condemned for actions that seem acceptable in men, for example, sacrificing home life for career ambitions, dominating and controlling a spouse's life, and fighting directly and strongly for their own needs and desires.

Western Ideas

From the beginnings of Western thought, a double standard has existed in regard to women and men. The idea of women's humanity as equivalent to men's, of men as equal sharers of domestic responsibilities, and of women and men as similarly good or bad has had little recognition in most people's writings or consciousness. As a result, distorted perceptions of women (and of men) over the years have created dislocations in female/male relationships.[2]

A first step is to recognize and disentangle these distortions, which have over the centuries translated into alienation, conflict, and unhappiness. Folkstories about marriage are unique in revealing how old these distortions are and how more realistic perceptions can foster more wholesome relations.

In today's world, many women are striving for equal recognition and equal acceptance with men in terms of their capacity for morality, nurturance, intelligence, or accomplishment. When each gender stereotypically sees a different and unrealistic set of attributes in the other, compatibility, intimacy, and harmony become difficult, if not impossible. By seeing women and men through the same lens, however, cooperation and reciprocity are more achievable. Folkstory marriage scenes provide keys to these important perceptions.

Marital Discord

We are rightly concerned about marital discord today. Changes in lifestyles have made it easier for unhappy couples to choose separation. Current attitudes of independence and self-actualization and the commercial availability of necessary goods and services have encouraged people to act out their disappointments. In earlier times the same sorrow would generally be borne in silence and secrecy inside one's home and one's psyche. The anguish remained even while the marriages lasted.

Today's marriages are more unstable because disillusioned spouses are more apt to walk out. The answer to this instability is not to suffer in silence as in the past. Suffering and anguish do not make for a good life. It is critical therefore to understand the nature of the dislocations that have existed for a long time and to find ways to improve married life in today's world.

We need to take a hard look at spouse relationships. We need to examine the actions of married partners to understand what goes on in the privacy of family life. We may then recognize what bodes well for marriage and how to make needed changes.

A major problem exists because we know so little about how spouses behave in everyday domestic life. Research about marriage has been based largely on self-reports, interviews, therapy sessions, surveys, responses to vignettes, and other similar methods.[3] These sources tell us what people say or what they want us to think, but not necessarily what they do. How many men will say, "I frequently punch my wife to get my own way"? Yet we know how prevalent wife abuse is. How many wives will say, "I nag and nag and nag till I get what I want"? Yet men will tell you how often they see and how much they dislike this behavior.

We need to learn more about marriage if we are to understand its dilemmas. According to Erich Fromm[4], unless we study the reasons for marital disharmony, we can hardly expect to make improvements.

Reflections of Marriage

Many students of human behavior (e.g., anthropologists, psychologists, psychiatrists) have stressed the critical importance of folkstories throughout human history. For centuries, even millenia, adults all over the world have told and listened to stories that uncovered for them the essence of human behavior. It is from this telling and retelling that people have focused on difficult situations, explored shared problems, sought solutions, and gained wisdom in dealing with their own lives.

These time-honored tales, designed originally for grown-ups, not children, remain a treasure trove for understanding human existence. They deal with a wide variety of basic human problems —the difficulties of growing up, the challenges of courtship, ways to become successful in one's work, and most important for our purpose, the nature of marriage and family relationships.

Included in the vast storehouse of folk literature are stories that shed light on the essence of wife-husband relationships. While technological progress has changed many areas of life, the basic nature of spouse interactions seems to have changed surprisingly little. Folkstories about wives and husbands remain a window into marriage relations and a mirror of our own life in today's world.

Focus of the Book

Stories retold in this book focus graphically on the interactions of married partners as they struggle with common problems[5]. From among hundreds of stories, I culled only those that illustrate marriage roles. Although in different collections similar stories are presented with different details, the essence of wife/husband relations remains the same. It is this essence that has been preserved and retold here in the stories of wives and husbands.

Specific scenes illustrate cultural, social, and psychological restraints that affect marital relations. They give us valuable models of behavior that help to distinguish between those that promote versus those that interfere with wholesome relationships. Thus stories are used to illustrate and to make comparisons with the work of theorists and researchers in family relations and help to sharpen our ability to improve married life.

I focused on several critical questions: What are the central issues facing married couples? How do wives act? Husbands? What happens to the wife? To the husband? Who is rewarded? Who is punished? Whose behavior changes? For what reason? What role do members of the community play?

Folkstories have not gone out of style. They continue to be published in great numbers, and they continue to hold important ideas for today's couples. They also help to put in perspective the contributions made to current thinking by feminist writers, marriage counselors, and family relations specialists. Domestic scenes show us that marriage has been a challenge for a very long time. We can learn from old stories where to start the journey to improve modern marriage.

Each chapter of this book addresses a different aspect of wife/husband relationships. We look at the following: what roles are available to wives and husbands; what is the nature of marital conflict; why is there so much spouse abuse; how does love fit into marriage; how does marriage differ in different cultures; and what can we do for a better future.

2
The Roles of Wives
and their Husbands

According to many recent writers, today's wives do not have an easy life. Carolyn Heilbrun[1] states that in recent literature marriage is frequently presented as a farce so far as women are concerned. Miriam Johnson[2] suggests that being a loving companion and an obedient wife are inherently incompatible; a woman cannot be both. Assessing the astounding statistics on wife battering, Jane Caputi[3] asserts that being a wife is an unsafe occupation. These writers thus recognize the difficulties today's women face in trying to fulfill conflicting demands: wifely compliance, domestic chores, outside job responsibilities, and personal satisfactions. Harris and Mc Namara[4] refer to the painful position of many wives who try to fit into culturally prescribed domestic roles which are ill-adapted to their personalities and talents. From the contemporary writings of Betty Friedan,[5] Gloria Steinem,[6] and Hochschild and Machung,[7] among others, one might assume that these dilemmas are of recent origin, arising from changes in 20th century life styles and the struggles for women's rights.

Folkstory scenes of marriage, however, challenge this conclusion. They show, on the contrary, that for centuries incompatible expectations, psychological tensions, and troubled marriage relationships have been the norm. Marital difficulties have endangered positive emotional ties and enjoyable shared experiences over the centuries, and have left a heritage of unsatisfactory marriage models. Thus despite many changes in the outside world, the psychological situation inside the home seems to have changed relatively little from earlier historical periods.

Instead of married bliss, wives and husbands continue to struggle with a wide variety of issues from the most trivial to the most monumental. Their behavior in modern marriage as in old folkstories exposes limitations in problem-solving skills as well as cultural, psychological and social requirements that interfere with loving relationships. Understanding the age-old scenes helps shed light on current marital dislocations.

Gender Roles in Marriage

How and why dissatisfactions arise in marriage are related to the kinds of roles wives and husbands are expected to fulfill. As Leichter and Mitchell[8] pointed out, these roles tend to conform to socially prescribed norms, which mold individual personalities and influence the marriages people have. Norms at different times and places often resemble each other, as Queen and Habenstein[9] have indicated in their study of family life in various cultures. Similarities in norms help explain similarities in people's behavior in different parts of the world.

Folkstory marriages reveal very few roles for wives and husbands. A similar finding about marriages today comes from the research of psychologist Howard Markman.[10] Role uniformity is also reminiscent of Beverly Stoeltje's work about the American frontier. She found only a few ways people could relate to each other given the challenges of frontier life.[11]

In folkstory scenes, spouses have a limited range of behaviors. Contrary to the already mentioned popular view of women as either good or bad, wives are seen in four possible roles: the Shrew, the Wise Woman, the Good Woman, and the Assertive Woman. Husbands also appear in four different roles: the Boss, the Tolerant Man, the Puppet, and the Assertive Man.[12] In today's world, Mildred Pollner[13] investigated how married people are presented in the media, both in print and on television, and found that marital behaviors continue to be similar to the roles found in folkstories.

Three of the four designations for wives (Shrew, Wise Woman, Good Woman) are often explicitly stated in printed collections.[14] The designations themselves are forms of cultural communication; they impose a value judgment on women's actions. Given the strong male influence in preserving folk literature,[15] it is not surprising that the judgments tend to be male-oriented. Many notions of women in today's world are seen also as reflecting male views.[16]

The characterizations of folkstory men as Boss, Tolerant Man, Puppet, or Assertive Man are based on the actions of the husbands themselves and not on any specific designations in the marriage scenes. The cultural message of most stories seems to be that women's behavior, more so than men's, needs to be revealed and corrected. This premise is a reflection of our long legal and social history of restricting the participation of women in many spheres of life and giving legal control to their husbands. This history has not been conducive to fair and equal relationships between women and men.

Many women in the past, though resentful of unfair restrictions, had little power to make changes. Today women have become more conscious and more openly critical of inequities. Notwithstanding the progress made in education and employment, however, the drive for equality inside the home has not met with great success.

Unequal Marriage Partners

Several marriage roles reveal fundamental sources of difficulty in married life. Marriages based on the inequality of spouses and the expectation of male dominance are commonplace and troublesome for both women and men. The wife copes as the Shrew, the Wise Woman, or the Good Woman; and the husband is seen as the Boss, the Tolerant Man, or the Puppet. The stories that follow illustrate their interrelationships.

The Shrew and the Boss

The most frequently presented wife in marriage scenes is the Shrew. The Shrew is a woman who possesses qualities considered repugnant and generally unacceptable to her husband. Women cast as Shrews are likely to be independent, determined, curious, ambitious, willful, disobedient, or insistent on their own way. In a struggle for power, the Shrew threatens her husband's rule of the household. She acts in a direct, confrontational manner, and leaves little doubt about her wishes. While she may be applauded by today's feminists, her actions are not prized in folkstories.

The stereotype of a traditional woman as a passive compliant creature is contradicted by the Shrew. This wife is forthright in action and quite able to express herself. While not a good woman, neither is the Shrew altogether bad. She need only change her attitude to be acceptable to her husband.

The following scenes reveal unacceptable aspects of the Shrew, qualities that are not prized by many husbands in today's marriages either. For example, the argumentative wife is seen in "The Woman Who Was Stubborn."

> It irked the old farmer that his wife knew how to read and he did not. He was often cross; she was often contrary. One day, the old man mentioned that he had to shave. His wife disagreed. Because he wore a beard, she told him the word was "clip" not "shave." The husband was incensed by her remark, and insisted he was right. The argument became long and heated; neither would give in. Having had enough, the husband dragged his wife to the river and pushed her in. Holding her head under the water, he yelled that she should say "shave." No longer able to speak and as a final gesture of defiance, she lifted her hand out of the water, and using two fingers like a scissors showed that the word was "clip."

The wife in this scene refused to be controlled by her husband. Her struggle was for the right to express her own opinion. The husband on the other hand expected to be dominant and was incensed by her greater knowledge as well as her disobedience. The scene shows how the conflict was resolved. Despite the husband's determination to control her actions, she was equally determined to preserve her individuality. This turned out to be a dangerous path. This wife could not adjust to the expected subservient wifely role. Although this scene occurred in olden times, it like others discussed below is applicable to many marriages in our own world. Many men become abusive of wives who are defiant and who may outshine them in accomplishment.[17]

Another Shrew is a woman considered to be inappropriately ambitious. "The Woman Who Would Be a Leader" is an example.

> A capable peasant woman wanted to fill the vacant position of leader of the *mir* [little village] where she lived. Her husband resented her ambition, but he could not stop her. She became the leader and acted very much as previous leaders had. She took bribes and delayed collecting taxes to appease some of the town's important *kulaks* [rich money-lending peasants]. After meetings of the Town Council, she would often go with the *kulaks* and drink at the local tavern. The *barin* [local nobleman], shocked at such behavior in a woman, sent a *cossack* [soldier] to look for her. Frightened, the woman hid in a sack to escape detection. When the

cossack came to her house, her husband stood aside while the *cossack* grabbed the sack and whipped the woman until she shrieked. After a good beating, she no longer wanted to be leader of the *mir*. She gave up her ambition, became a good wife, and obeyed her husband.

Although the husband did not overtly thwart his wife's ambition, he was nevertheless a willing accomplice to prevent her success. Acquiescing to the *cossack*'s attack, the husband was able to achieve his goal. Recent writers[18] have indicated that today a women's career ambitions often create difficulties in domestic relationships. As the above story indicates, this situation has been a problem for a long time.

Some Shrews are independent women whose lives contain a secret aspect, as in "The Woman Who Was a Bird."

After his first wife died, a man met a lovely young woman and married her. He did not know that his new wife was really a bird in disguise. His young son observed that when his father was away his stepmother sang some magic verses and changed into her original form, a bird. Just before his father returned, she sang a special song and changed back into a beautiful woman.

The son told his father about this transformation. The shocked man could not believe what he heard. To verify the son's story, he began to sing the same magic verses very loud. To his surprise, the woman began to change into a bird. The indignant husband immediately took his gun and shot her.

This wife tried to resolve the conflict between her culturally defined role and who she really was. Her solution was to be her true self when her husband was away and conform to her wifely role when he came home. But the world, in the guise of the man's son, would not allow that resolution, and neither would the husband. Like the "Woman Who Was Stubborn" above, this woman suffered from the same painful position that many wives do today. Currently, many women choose to assume different personae for their career and their domestic roles, often with attendant psychological and interpersonal dislocations.[19]

Shrews may also be nosy and nagging, qualities very much disliked by their husbands. "The Woman Who Was Too Curious" shows this kind of woman.

A husband received the gift of understanding the language of animals, but he was warned that he would die if he revealed this secret. He then began to laugh whenever he heard the animals talk. His wife became very curious about his strange behavior, but of course he refused to tell her. She nagged him incessantly to learn his secret. Unable to stand her haranguing any longer, he became frightened and distraught. The rooster in the yard, noticing his plight, began to ridicule him for his inaction. The rooster suggested that there are ways to make a wife obey. The husband took the hint. He then took a whip from the wall and beat his wife into unconsciousness. When she regained consciousness, the woman no longer cared why her husband laughed. And she gave up being curious.

This husband felt he owed his wife no explanation for his apparently peculiar behavior. However, he was greatly distressed and even felt endangered by her insistent questioning. Although he had no intention of harming her, the outside world in the guise of the rooster intervened and taught him the culturally approved way of dealing with an intractable woman. The story reveals the harm that can result from a lack of trust and of honest communication between spouses. Deborah Tannen,[20] in her popular book, *You Just Don't Understand*, stressed that communication problems remain a source of trouble in many modern households.

Instead of merely having an unpleasant personality, a few Shrews are truly bad women who harm or plan to harm others. The wife in "The Woman Who Was Evil" is this kind of woman.

An old witch, angry at the local Prince for punishing her mother, transformed herself into a beautiful woman and tried to convince the Prince to marry her. Since his first wife had died and left him with a small daughter, he agreed. The new wife, wanting to punish the Prince, continually found fault with the child and finally buried her in a hole near a rose bush. The bush sang a strange melody when anyone approached, telling of the child buried underneath. One day the distraught Prince walked by and heard the song. Outraged, he took a shovel, dug up the little girl, and buried his wife instead.

The woman in this story is shown as clearly an evil person, while the husband is presented as the most powerful person in the household. He is the sole protector of the family and the one allowed to impose punishment, including death, on family members.

In stories as in the world around us, when the wife is called a Shrew, she is accorded little sympathy or understanding. The Shrew is generally disapproved of, and as in the Shakespeare play, the husband is rewarded for taming her. Most folkstory Shrews are controlled by domineering husbands (Bosses) who frequently resort to violence and threats. If the women are incorrigible, they may be destroyed by men, who are not held accountable for the crime. The above scenes illustrate Jane Caputi's[21] judgment that wifehood is an unsafe occupation. Three wives were killed and two beaten into submission, typical resolutions in stories about Shrews.

The Shrew and the Tolerant Man

A few shrewish women are married to men who are tolerant and can adapt to life with a Shrew. The marriage of the Shrew and the Tolerant Man, however, is always presented as an undesirable arrangement. An example is "The Woman Who Ruled the Household."

> A meek rabbi was able to get along with his shrewish domineering wife. Members of his community were greatly distressed and urged him to get rid of her. The whole town was upset because they cared about the rabbi. The rabbi explained that God had given this woman to him because he had the patience and forbearance to cope with her. If another man, unable to tolerate her, had married her, it would have ruined both their lives.

Even though the rabbi seemed quite able to cope with his dominating and probably disobedient wife, people in the community found the situation intolerable and felt the need to intervene. In this case, the rabbi had great concern and compassion for his wife. He also recognized that few men share his unusual view.

Many men today face the quandary of trying to accept the idea of equality in spouse relations and at the same time of fulfilling the cultural expectation to be the ruler of the household. The conflict, often discussed in today's world, nevertheless has its counterpart in similar situations from times long past.

Most folkstory Shrews survive by being forced to change into compliant Good Women. Shrews who do not change their personalities are those married to Tolerant Men or those who are killed by their Boss husbands.

The Wise Woman and the Puppet

Wives as Wise Women are able to accomplish their goals, especially when trying to correct their husbands' faults. Husbands may be arrogant, foolhardy, weak, or behaving contrary to cultural norms. To correct these defects, the Wise Woman succeeds through indirect methods rather than direct confrontation. Deceiving her husband is very common. He is the Puppet who ultimately does what his wife wants. He thinks he dominates the household, while his wife skillfully maneuvers him according to her wishes. These feminine wiles are by no means unknown in today's world. "The Woman Who Changed Her Husband" illustrates this marriage.

> A wealthy man preferred his friends to his poor younger brother. The wealthy man's wife was upset by her husband's disregard of family loyalty and tried without success to reunite the two brothers. She finally thought of a ruse. She convinced her husband that she killed a traveler who she thought was a thief. Now realizing her mistake and terrified that she would be apprehended, she begged him to save her. The husband decided to ask his friends for help, but he was gravely disappointed when they refused. At his wife's urging, he asked his brother to help him bury the body and to keep the situation a secret. The brother was shocked, but promptly agreed to help. The husband's friends then asked him for money to keep silent. That made him even angrier at them, and he refused. The friends reported him to the district magistrate, who ordered the couple to appear before him. Upon questioning, the wife revealed that the wrapped body was a dead dog. She had used the ruse to demonstrate the difference between the friends and the brother. The magistrate punished the bribe-seeking friends and praised the wife. The husband established a close and proper relationship with his younger brother and appreciated his wife's wisdom.

The Wise Woman, while a much less prevalent figure in marriage stories than the Shrew, is nevertheless a familiar character. These wives can fool, pretend, divert, masquerade, lie, and trick in order to be successful. The Puppet does not complain of his wife's tactics. On the contrary, he is proud of her wisdom and happy to get the benefits of her management. These marriages, however, may well be described in Carolyn Heilbrun's[22] term—a farce.

Wise Woman stories have something in common with other farces—those of male tricksters, in which the weak outwit the strong. An important difference is that Wise Women cannot afford to revel publicly in their success, as male tricksters tend to do. For peace in the home, they must allow husbands to retain a public image of being dominant in the relationship. In addition, male tricksters tend to scheme for their own good, while the machinations of Wise Women are usually aimed at improving the husband for his own good. When women scheme for themselves in the stories, they are seen as Shrews.

Wise Wives are often referred to in today's world as the power behind the throne, or "behind every successful man is a smart wife."

The Good Woman and the Boss

The Good Woman, a wife who finds no fault with her husband, is shown as a male ideal. She is the accepting, acquiescent woman, who believes her husband can do no wrong. Subservient to his rule, she will fulfill whatever he requires of her. The Good Woman is always married to a Boss. A benevolent Boss can easily turn into a hostile one if he believes that his Good Woman has become a Shrew. "The Woman Who Lost Her Beauty" is an example.

> A king influenced by his Prime Minister went to observe for himself the beauty of the wife of one of his courtiers. The king arranged to keep the courtier at court while he visited the wife. The woman's trusted servant, suspecting some unsavory plan, allowed the king to look at the woman only from the distance while she was walking in the garden. He was so moved by her beauty that upon leaving he left a small gift behind. Returning home later, the husband was greatly angered to see an anonymous gift for his wife. Suspecting her of infidelity, he began to shun her, treating her with disdain and indifference. The woman, unaware of what had happened and confused and heartsick at her husband's behavior, pined away and lost her beauty. When the Prime Minister realized what had happened, he told the

king of the woman's plight. Saddened, the king informed
the courtier of his indiscretion, and praised the virtuous
woman and her faithful servant. The husband went home
delighted with the good wife he had.

Examples of Good Women reinforce compliance in women and
control by men. The Good Woman resembles the stereotypic beautiful-
passive woman discussed at some length by such writers as Madonna
Kolbenschlag,[23] Ethel Phelps,[24] and many others. But while this woman
is usually pursued and respected in courtship, she is subjugated and
controlled in marriage. A somewhat similar situation has recently been
recounted about Diana, the Princess of Wales. In Andrew Morton's[25]
well received biography, Diana's ill health is ascribed to the psychological difficulties of complying with the rigorous requirements of regal
life plus dealing with an apparently uncaring and philandering husband,
Prince Charles. Ironically, the Princess's life may aptly be called a
"fairy tale marriage."

When tormented by the Boss, the Good Woman suffers physical
and psychological harm. For her forbearance, however, she is eventually appreciated by her husband and rewarded by others in the community. However, the Good Woman illustrates Miriam Johnson's[26] belief that
a woman cannot be both a loving companion and an obedient wife. The
compliant Good Woman is rarely presented as a companion to her husband, and behaving with blind obedience leaves little room for mature
love.

Subversion

The word "subvert" is defined in the *The American College
Dictionary* as follows:

   1. to overthrow something existing or established;
   2. to cause the downfall, ruin, or destruction of;
   3. to undermine the principles of; to corrupt.[27]

The word subversion is usually applied to political activities, and
its application to marriage underscores the feminist principle that
indeed "the personal is political." It is precisely in the personal relations
between wife and husband that the politics of gender are acted out.

In the Household

Marriage scenes discussed above show a variety of unsatisfying
relationships. These marriages are disappointing for those seeking com-

panionship and happiness. Wives are particularly in danger because of the cultural requirement of a controlling domineering husband and the acceptance of the use of force against women.

The Shrew is severely punished for her contrariness. She may be beaten, killed, or at the very least condemned by the community. The Wise Woman has to be especially skilled at deviousness and deception to be successful. This requires courage, daring and luck. The Good Woman suffers indignities at the hands of her husband and is powerless to help herself. These roles do not illustrate mature adult women respected by husbands and other people. The wives who try to maintain their independence and integrity tend to be destroyed.

The unfortunate message of these stories is that for the women and the marriages to survive, albeit rather unhappily, the wife needs to be subverted.

Of the Wife
In the interplay between women and men, each of the above definitions of *subvert* has meaning for a different type of wife.

1. To overthrow something existing or established:
The Shrew in folkstories has to be overthrown. Shrews and Bosses are very similar. Both use direct confrontation. Each is clear in what she/he wants, and pursues a clear direction to accomplish her/his goal. These qualities are severely condemned in the woman while they are applauded in the man.

The Shrew is not valued for strength and purposefulness, as the Boss is. Her forthrightness, direct confrontation, and clarity of purpose are in fact to be subverted.

To facilitate the process, these qualities are first described in pejorative terms—the woman is a nag, contrary, stubborn, a Shrew. Once she is seen negatively, the Shrew must be overthrown. Miriam Johnson[28] makes a similar point about our own society. We uphold the norm of male dominance in part through the use of such epithets as henpecked husbands, battleaxes, and castrating bitches.

Name calling helps to justify whatever abuse is necessary to force the Shrew to give up her unpleasant qualities. She is expected to subvert her personality, to overthrow her existing way of behaving, and become something she is not, to change into a compliant acquiescent woman. In most Shrew stories either she changes or she is killed. The only Shrews who remain true to themselves and survive are those with Tolerant Men as husbands. In this case, both husband and wife live with public criticism. They do not fit the required cultural ideal of a dominant man and a subservient woman. While men are not expected to subvert their confrontational and dominant qualities, women are.

2. To cause the downfall, ruin, destruction of:

The Good Woman suffers temporary ruin or total destruction as a result of her husband's intransigeance and lack of trust.[29] The Good Woman has to abase herself to demonstrate her acquiescence and compliance. Good Women become psychologically distorted. Whatever good sense they may have had in the past tends to be ruined and destroyed in their complete acceptance of a husband's often strange or cruel behavior. Good Women do not seem to be mature adults. They appear akin to children, and are treated by their husbands more as appreciated servants than as partners in life.

The Good Woman suffers ruin and destruction. Her health may be destroyed, her appearance ruined, and her psychological well-being subverted by her husband's neglect and withdrawal of love.

Many Good Women suffer in silence. However, in the end they are usually restored to the husbands' good graces. Whatever independence they may have once possessed has disappeared, and any shred of individuality is no longer there. On the other hand, domineering husbands of Good Women are quite acceptable in the stories despite the harm they may inflict.

3. To undermine the principles of; to corrupt:

The Wise Woman is corrupted in her marital relationship, and her ethical principles are undermined. Though in most other respects she can be a fine, upstanding, and intelligent person, this wife must stoop to various types of underhanded activities to accomplish her goals. Wise Women become liars, manipulators, deceivers—all in an effort to influence the behavior of their husbands. Male tricksters in other stories resemble Wise Wives in the use of underhanded tactics and strategy. A major difference is that male tricksters struggle with unjust outside forces such as powerful political figures, giants, or supernatural spirits, and win some measure of fairness and independence for themselves. Wise Women, on the other hand, use trickery in dealing with the person to whom they are closest, their husbands, and generally for the husband's benefit. People tend to resort to underhanded methods when they are powerless to address their grievances directly; when, as Lawrence Levine[30] puts it, "conditions permitting the application of . . . moral values [are] absent." The fact that women become tricksters in marriage reveals the difficulty a wife often has in pursuing honest, direct dealings with her husband.

Marriage scenes emphasize that Wise Wife behavior is laudable, effective, and valuable. It is a prescription for a wife's success in marriage. The Wise Woman, however, has been subverted by having her principles undermined and her morals corrupted.

Of the Husband

Wives are not the only ones subverted. Husbands also suffer from the corrupting influence of their position.

Instead of men acting as sources of strength and righteousness, we find husbands stooping to behavior they would avoid in other areas of life. In most masculine physical battles, the accepted ethical principle is to "pick on someone your own size." A man is considered a bully if he attacks and beats another who is smaller, weaker, handicapped, and generally less able to compete in the conflict. This in no way applies when a husband attacks his wife. The fact that she is generally smaller, physically weaker, sometimes pregnant, and less skilled in physical violence fades in importance compared to the goal of getting her to do what he wants.

Another tenet of masculine morality is "facing the consequences like a man." Yet husbands are not called to account for actions that are clearly immoral and illegal. Punishments or even criticisms are rarely meted out in the stories to men who torment, beat, injure, or even murder their wives.

As Evelyn White[31] points out, a man (as the Boss) is psychologically harmed when he is rewarded for treating a wife with cruelty, disdain and contempt. Contrary to moral teaching, he is often excused from even the most serious transgression without so much as a mention of the crime. His sense of right and wrong is corrupted by the social approval given to the physical and psychological abuse he inflicts on his wife.

The Tolerant Man is unable to enjoy his role as a patient, caring, understanding person. He is reminded that his behavior goes against the cultural norm. He must become either a tyrannical figure subverting his own personality, or remain true to himself and suffer the disdain of others. Neither is a psychologically comfortable resolution.

The Puppet finds that his difficulties can be solved by someone else, his wife. He is relieved of the responsibility to correct his own undesirable behavior. While grateful for a Wise Woman, he nevertheless is self-centered and blind to his ownshortcomings. In addition, the

Puppet shows little concern for ethics as he accepts the rewards of his wife's underhandedness. He seems unconcerned or unaware that his need to appear dominant has encouraged his wife's unethical behavior.

Of the General Public

There is one further subversion that needs to be mentioned—the subversion of the general public. The way in which rewards and punishments are meted out subverts everyone's sense of fairness and justice.

In marriage scenes, rewards and punishments are determined not by actions but by gender. What is rewarded in men is punished in women; what is praised in women is condemned in men. This double standard has meaning only in terms of the underlying rationale. Whatever bolsters men's power and control of the household is rewarded; whatever encourages women's subservience and compliance is likewise rewarded. Contrary to what we are normally taught, behavior in itself has no right and wrong. We are asked to condone beatings, torment, and even murder, if used to bring women to obey. We are asked to accept unethical behavior if used to preserve male dominance. Even where husbands have mistakenly accused their wives of wrongdoing, they are not usually held accountable for their mistakes. Thus, we are all taken in and asked to subvert our normal sense of fairness and justice.

This was clearly demonstrated in a class of adult students I taught recently. I told the story, "The Woman Who Was Stubborn" (see page 8) to the class, and then asked for comments. Students recognized that the wife's crime included stubbornness, independence, contrariness, and foolishness. And her punishment? Drowning. In regard to the husband, his crime also was seen in the same light—stubbornness, inflexibility, and stupidity. Only after several moments did one student finally add "Murder!" The class sat in dumbfounded silence, startled at their casual acceptance of the husband's cruelty as normal, in essence a subversion of their own moral sense.

Comments on Subversion

In most marriage stories and in many marriages today, subversion of both the wife and the husband is needed to insure male dominance/female subservience. Most currently published folkstories about marriage tend to reinforce the persistent idea of gender inequality. The way in which most spouses deal with each other leaves much to be desired in the development of respectful, caring, intimate relations.

Both spouses are harmed by the unequal relationship in which they find themselves. And the public perceiving these scenes as lessons in behavior is harmed as well.

It is no wonder that wives do not have a happy life. It is psychologically distressing to be forced into subverting one's personality, to be subservient in what should be a sharing relationship, to give up one's individuality, and to act in ways that contradict one's own ethical values. These unfortunate contradictions in role requirements help explain the high rates of mental and physical illness among married women. Modern writers are beginning to debunk the myth of marital happiness, to uncover the long-denied hazards of wifehood, and to look at the reality of many present-day spouse relationships, which are echoes of what we have found in many folkstories of past marriages.

Assertive Spouses

There are a few heartwarming stories of marital devotion, harmony, and compatibility. Just as happy marriages exist in some homes, so they also exist in some stories.

Spouse relationships in these situations are a notable departure from the distortions and subversions discussed above. For want of a better term, I have called these spouses Assertive Women and Assertive Men.[32]

The Assertive Woman in folkstories is surprisingly like the Shrew. This woman clearly states what she wants, is forthright in her dealing with her husband, and is not afraid to disagree with him. The difference is in the way she is treated. One is reminded of Eliza Doolittle's comment in Shaw's play, *Pygmalion*, that a lady is identified not by how she acts but by how others act toward her. This is the case with the Assertive Woman. Instead of being scorned for her forthright qualities, she is appreciated, accepted, and treated with respect. Her husband, an Assertive Man, reveals the same forthright dealings. "The Woman Who Changed Her View" is an example of a marriage of Assertive Spouses.

> A young man loved his wife and got for her whatever gifts she desired. Jealous women taunted her, saying that if he really loved her, he would get her the Magic Cloth of the Serpent. This thought made the wife unhappy and gloomy. Although she was silent on the subject, her husband insisted on knowing the cause of her unhappiness. She finally admitted her wish for the Magic Cloth. Concerned for her

happiness, he was willing to face the great dangers involved in retrieving the Cloth. With instructions from a wise old woman, he overcame the dangers and captured the famous item. Bringing the Magic Cloth back to his wife, he recounted the perils of his journey and repeated the old woman's advice to be satisfied with what you have. Frightened by her husband's narrow escapes and impressed with the old woman's words, the wife no longer listened to gossipy neighbors and was satisfied with the accomplishments of her loving husband.

The above theme of a man overcoming obstacles for a woman he loves is more typical of courtship than of marriage scenes. When this theme does appear, it is in marriages of Assertive Spouses. In the above scene, even though the wife was overly concerned with community gossip, her husband valued her wishes and was respectful of her. He did not denigrate or ridicule her, and he did not beat her to change her views. His efforts to accommodate her, dangerous though they were, were rewarded by a future of compatibility and harmony with his wife. The woman's views ultimately changed, but not through harshness and violence. The story shows her ability to evaluate in a new light what is important in life. Other Assertive Wives and Husbands are also respectful and caring in marriage despite differences that exist between the pair. A story that has a sad outcome is "The Woman Who Couldn't Explain."

A handsome young man from another town met a young woman who appealed to him. He asked to speak to her parents about their marrying. Saying she had no relatives, the woman nevertheless agreed to become his wife on one condition. She insisted that he should not make any inquiries about her family. Although he did not understand this request, he recognized that it was important to her, and he readily agreed. After many years and many children, they held a large initiation feast for their first-born son. On that occasion, the husband was so perplexed at the absence of his wife's family that he asked about it. Realizing that his question spelled disaster, the woman became frantic. A great storm and earthquake ensued, and husband, wife, and children were buried in the disaster.

Although the mystery about the woman's family was not revealed, love and harmony prevailed for a long time. The story illustrates, however, that respecting a spouse's wishes without complete understanding has its limits. The message is underscored by the fact that the husband's momentary lapse turned out to be fatal. The story further demonstrates that the welfare of the whole family is dependent on trust between wife and husband. The tragedy in this story turns on the secrecy required and the resulting lack of open communication between the spouses.

These and other stories of Assertive Spouses revolve around the maintenance of marital harmony rather than control of the household. The Assertive Woman is recognized as an adult entitled to her own opinions and behavior. She is not presented in a negative light, and unlike the Shrew, she is acceptable to her husband and to others. The issues Assertive Spouses face are similar to those of other couples, but the attitudes and solutions are distinctly different. Assertive Couples do not resort to the use of force, verbal abuse or trickery. They try to understand and be thoughtful in dealing with each other as they seek suitable solutions to their difficulties.

These stories also illustrate that marriage is beset with problems, and that even with the best intentions, calamities happen. Yet they portray spouses who do not blame each other for misfortune, nor do the spouses force or manipulate each other to gain control. They exhibit a more communal than individualistic attitude, a greater emphasis on equal responsibility in marriage, and at the same time a respect for the differences between married partners.

Assertive Spouses operate in a cultural or personal environment that does not emphasize gender inequality. Bolstering male dominance is not required. Spouses act in straightforward ways and remain true to themselves. There is no reason for them to use subterfuge, and no gender difference exists in the judgment of their actions. These are spouses who are not subverted.

Marriage scenes of Assertive Spouses resemble the *strong families* that Stinnett and De Frain[33] found in their search for modern egalitarian marriages. It is interesting that the qualities making for harmonious marriages in earlier times are similar to those many spouses strive for today, often with great difficulty.

3

Partners in Domestic Conflict

Contradictions between the ideals of marriage and its reality exist in both life and story. Anticipating the joys of wedded bliss, courtship tends to encourage the belief that happiness in marriage is all but guaranteed. And of course in stories, Cinderella and her Prince, Snow White and her Rescuer, Rapunzel and her Tower-Climber, and a host of other couples are predicted to live "happily ever after."

These predictions are echoed in scholarly and popular notions of conjugal harmony, and attributed to a variety of causes. Mary Ryan[1] suggests that the ideal of conjugal love was present in an earlier American agrarian period when cooperation and sharing were required to keep the home functioning. William Goode[2] sees the rise of industrialization as encouraging greater companionship and intimacy between spouses. Miriam Johnson finds in the rise of Protestantism "a new dignity and more equality" for women and the encouragment of spouses to be "friends and lovers to each other."[3] Erich Fromm refers to the many articles on modern marriage that describe the ideal of a "smoothly functioning team."[4]

The Emergence of Conflict

Marriage experiences often contradict these notions, and reveal many dislocations in married life. Conflict is a central issue and conflict resolution the lesson to be learned.

A striking illustration of marriage behavior appears in "The Woman and Her Husband Who Were Silent." Here we see highlighted the difference between courtship and marriage through a scene that occurs immediately after the wedding ceremony. Its message is typical of many marriages.

> As soon as the last wedding guest left, the newly married couple hastened to be alone in their new home. Amidst their excitement, they forgot to shut the door. The bride then asked her husband to close the door. He was surprised and somewhat bothered by the request, and suggested that she do this herself. She was taken aback and promptly refused.
>
> Not having faced this kind of problem before, they finally agreed on a test of wills. They would not speak to each other at all, and the first one to break the silence would have to shut the door. So they sat in silence in their wedding outfits all night long. And the door remained open.
>
> During the night, thieves were delighted to see the open door and entered. The bride and groom marshalled all their will power and remained silent. The thieves helped themselves to whatever they could carry and left. In the morning, the police looked in and saw the ransacked house. Checking on the trouble, they tried in vain to get one or the other to tell what had happened. But neither one would speak. Frustrated, the police threatened to strike the husband if he did not answer.
>
> The wife broke the silence, begging the police not to harm her new mate. Thereupon the triumphant husband shouted, " I won! You have to shut the door!"

This scene, which begins right after the wedding, reveals much about the nature of marital conflict. Unlike courtship, where two young people have the same aims and try to please each other, these recently married spouses become immediate rivals for control of the household. The husband seems to be a fool and the wife a stubborn woman, and we may be tempted to dismiss the scene as the idiocy of a spoiled young couple.

But this story is widely distributed and told in many areas of the world.[5] Therefore, there may be more to the message than so superficial an interpretation.

Several aspects of the new relationship need attention. First, the scene takes place as soon as the wedding party is over. Obviously, even before the physical consummation of the marriage, the psychological transition from courtship to marriage may begin. The issue is a seemingly trivial one—who should close the door. Each spouse, however, sees in that act a loss of status in both the outside world and within the household. One could imagine that in courtship, each partner would have hurried to close the door to be more acceptable in the eyes of the other. But in marriage, when acceptance has been assured, the act of door closing takes on a different meaning.

Each spouse puts her/his honor on the line in refusing to do the other's bidding. But what, one may ask, is dishonorable about doorclosing? Is it the act itself, or is it the question of who controls the behavior of the other? If we look at the scene in terms of power and control, we see an early struggle for ruling the household though over quite a ridiculous issue.

But controlling the household is not a ridiculous issue. It is too often the basis of difficulties in many marriages. The need to win, to be the one whose wishes are obeyed, often supersedes other aspects of married life.

In the above scene, we see that controlling the action is more important to each spouse than wealth (the thieves took whatever they wanted with no interference); more important than safety and exposure to public ridicule (they sat mutely with the door wide open all night); more important than comfort (they did not eat, drink, or even move from their seats); more important than sex (they did not consummate the marriage); and for the husband, more important than pain and suffering (the police were going to beat him). The conflict is resolved because the wife, out of sympathy, speaks to prevent her husband from being hurt. At that point, her concern for his welfare becomes more important than her desire to get her own way. The husband, however, expresses no gratitude or appreciation of his wife's concern. He simply exults that his power has prevailed.

The story is unique for revealing how quickly this struggle may set in and the length to which marriage partners will go to win. Even the title is symbolic; the struggle for power is rarely admitted openly, but is a silent underlying force in many marriages.

More recently, an urban legend echoed a similar message. A prospective groom was informed by a relative that if he spoke to his bride right after the wedding ceremony before she spoke to him, he would be assured of future control of the household. Eager to act on this advice, after the wedding ceremony he was about to whisper, "You look lovely," but his new wife turned to him and said, "Don't step on my train."

In one way or another this theme of winning pervades a great many marriages. Marriage is often a covert struggle or overt warfare rather than peaceful bliss.

A recent bumper sticker proclaims, "War does not decide who is right, only who is left." In this chapter, we look at domestic conflicts and assess what and who are left at the end of the struggle.

Marriage-as-War

In warring marriages, winning is everything. Most spouses are motivated to control and to change the other's behavior.

The reasons for conflict may range from trivial to critical. The issue may be as inconsequential as how one drinks milk or as serious as cuckolding a husband.

"The Woman Who Liked Bread in Milk" shows an attack on a wife for an innocuous remark.

> A poor old couple earned their livelihood by begging from village to village. Becoming very thirsty, the husband said he planned to ask for milk in the next village. The wife had some dry bread in her pocket and remarked that she would like to crumble it into the milk. The husband, who preferred plain milk, responded by scolding her harshly and beating her. It was all in vain. When they got to the next village, no one would give them anything.

By contrast, in "The Woman Who Saved Her Lover," a serious offense is presented in a humorous vein.

> A wealthy man was married to a beautiful wife. The wife preferred the attentions of a younger man, whom she took as a lover. They had a special signal, which informed the lover when it was safe to come to the woman. One night, the signal was accidentally set the wrong way, and the lover arrived at her home at an inopportune time. The husband, at home with his wife, became suspicious and angry. He was about to reach for a heavy club when his wife convinced him that an evil spirit had knocked on the door. She begged him to cast a spell on the spirit by reciting special verses with her. When her husband had shouted the verses loud

enough for the lover to hear, the wife claimed that the spirit had gone, and they were safe. The lover went home amused and waited for a better time.

Obviously neither of the above scenes is designed to illustrate justice, fairness, or respect in interpersonal relations. The degree of seriousness of the issue makes little difference.

In "The Woman Who Liked Bread in Milk," there seems no connection between the wife's desire to put bread in the milk and her husband's beating her. He is not chastised or accountable in any way. What can be deduced is that enforcing his will, even capriciously, is acceptable, and violence is the way to do it.

"The Woman Who Saved her Lover" makes light of a serious transgression. Had the woman used deception for her husband's benefit, she would have been lauded as a Wise Woman. Here, however, she is a sly Shrew since her purpose was to help herself and her lover.

Morality and accountability are suspended. The more important lesson relates to methods of wresting and keeping control of the household. Who wins and how become more relevant than what is argued about.

Wise Woman and Good Woman behaviors illustrate ways around open conflict. While not in direct struggle, these wives choose covert ways of handling differences. One example is "The Woman Who Turned into a Leopard."

> A man and a woman on a long journey became very hungry and thirsty. The man suggested that the woman change into a leopard and catch an animal for food. Upset by this request but not seeking an argument, the woman turned into a leopard and leaping near her husband, frightened him badly. Terrified, he climbed a tree and stayed there until she changed back into her human form. Chastising her husband, she said, "It is a man's place to hunt animals for food, not a woman's."

This Wise Woman taught her husband an important lesson through an unexpected response to his request.

The Good Woman offers no challenge at all. Her husband wins with little or no conflict. As the Boss, he rules his wife and the household, and the wife often tolerates abasing treatment in the hope of being prized by her husband. "The Woman Who Was Innocent" shows the difficulties a Good Woman may face.

> A poor peasant went off to war, leaving his young wife and their small son. While he was away, to comfort the child, the wife showed him her shadow on the wall, instructing him to greet that shadow every night as his father. One day, the husband unexpectedly returned from the war. After a warm greeting, the wife went into the garden to gather food for their meal. Meanwhile, the child told his father of another father who came every night. Suspecting his wife of infidelity, the jealous husband berated and abused her when she returned. She begged and pleaded with him to reveal the cause of his anger. She protested her innocence and reaffirmed her fidelity to him. To no avail. He beat her and drove her from the house. That evening, when the child saw his father's shadow on the wall, he turned and greeted it, as his mother had instructed. The husband then realized his great mistake. By this time, however, the distraught woman, unaware of the source of his anger, had drowned herself to prove her innocence, as is the practice in her country. The anguished husband prayed that her soul recognize his repentance and find peace.

In these overt and covert marriage struggles, there is little understanding, discussion, compromise or negotiation to resolve a conflict. Neither spouse seems to explain her/his side of the issue. Each spouse instead is on an individual journey to personal triumph. In a similar vein, scholars have noted the prevalence of overt and covert marital conflict as significant patterns among present day spouses.[6]

The saying, "Everything's fair in love and war," seems appropriate in both courtship and marriage. In courtship, ethics and morality may be suspended for the young couple to succeed in their quest for each other. In marriage, on the other hand, morals and ethics may be suspended to allow one spouse to win over the other one in the domestic war.

Given that many marriages are a struggle of wills in a cultural situation that requires male dominance/female subservience, it is easy to understand why the roles of wives and husbands vary so little. Women's choices are limited to direct struggle (Shrew), underhanded manipulation (Wise Wife), or complete surrender (Good Woman). Men can be the forceful controller (Boss), the figurehead (Puppet), or the subjugated victim (Tolerant Man).

Many spouses seem more distant and more isolated from each other at the end of the conflict than they were at the beginning. The Shrew has learned not to reveal her true self. The Wise Wife has learned that conniving pays off. The Good Woman has found reinforcement for her self-abasement. The Bosses are often supported in their disregard for their wives' welfare; the Puppet has learned that his wife's machinations can do him good; and the Tolerant Man continues to live with dissatisfaction and community disapproval.

Those who are left are not the most attractive people. We see the subservient wife and the conniving one; the violent husband and the manipulated one; and the unacceptable Shrew and Tolerant Man. These people are generally not more understanding, more capable of intimacy or mutuality, or more likely to enjoy a happy relationship. Were they living in today's world, many of the women would probably have opted for divorce or seen psychiatrists long since. Confused by and often denying the contradictions of married life, women become the subordinates and losers in what they expected would be a life of caring, sharing, and love.

Marriage Without War

But not every marriage is a struggle of wills. In sharp contrast, scenes that bypass the overt or covert marriage-as-war metaphor are those of Assertive Spouses. In these marriages, neither winning nor male dominance is prized. Spouses are not out to change the other, but instead exhibit caring and respectful behavior toward each other.

Assertive Spouses do not have to choose between ruling or being ruled. Where there is disagreement, Assertive Wives and Husbands have the self-esteem to explain their own position in a direct manner, without deriding, degrading or attacking their partners. "The Woman Who Lost Her Father" illustrates a respectful spouse relationship even though the story does not end happily.[7]

A happy couple's life together was destroyed after the husband had received a gift of understanding animal language. He was warned that if he told anyone of this gift, he would die. This made for a serious dilemma. When the wife's father died, she misinterpreted her husband's laughter, caused by something the animals said, as mocking her grief. His efforts to reassure her were unsuccessful because he could not explain the reason for his laughter. Finally, finding no other way to convince her of his devotion, the husband told her the truth, and thereby lost his life. The wife was saddened that her curiosity and misinterpretation had resulted in her husband's death.

The basic premise of this scene, that a husband accepts a gift that he cannot disclose even to his wife, sets the stage for tragedy. The husband, facing a dilemma, chooses death rather than destroy his wife's faith in him. The idea of using conflict and force to stop her demands and thus create a hostile marriage is not an option for him. The story indicates that the maintenance of mutual love and respect can be more precious than life itself.

Conclusion

The maturity of Assertive Couples contrasts sharply with the vying for power of other partners. From the point of view of enhancing marital relations and improving spouse equality, it would seem that wives and husbands who are at war with each other have much to learn from the stories of Assertive Spouses.

4
Descent into Violence

One of the greatest dangers facing folkstory wives is that of being beaten by their husbands. Violent assault, normally considered a criminal act among men, is treated as a casual part of daily life in many folkstory households. Pauline Bart explains:

> Patriarchy encourages male violence against women . . . by legitimizing men's rights to control women . . .Poetic imagery and feminist analyses together will help us to see and understand the meaning of the endemic, unexceptional, but shocking amount of violence in all women's lives.[1]

The poetic imagery and feminist analysis of folkstory texts illuminate for us the enormity of violence against women. Marriage scenes help us to fathom the nature and meaning of this widespread violence.

Statistical compilations, shocking as they are,[2] do not reveal the far reaching personal effects of wife abuse; and personal accounts are hampered by problems of memory recall, self-conscious explanations, concern for pride and appearances, and worry over future dangers from present accusations. Also, scholarly research cannot recreate the actual scenes of domestic violence.

Folkstories on the other hand unveil details of a wide array of abuse situations. As the plot unfolds, we begin to understand motivating factors, contributing circumstances, and precipitating incidents that are involved in abuse situations. The stories provide an opportunity to witness the development and onset of violence, the victimization that occurs in households, and the results of these harmful events.

Although many men in folkstory texts resort to physical attacks on their wives, only some are portrayed as brutal by nature. Many husbands start out as Tolerant Men. Yet in order to rule their wives, they become the Boss and use physical and psychological abuse, generally successful means of control.

Abuse stories often end with the prediction that the spouses will now get along well, indicating that a beating convinces a woman to give in to her husband. Women, unable to withstand the effects of brutality, capitulate. Folkstories contain important truths about wife battering.[3]

Society Expects Wife Abuse

Wife abuse is present in a very large number of folkstories about marriage. These stories are published repeatedly with no editorial comment on the unpunished crimes that are committed. Their very existence in collections without critical comment is a silent acceptance of the stories having educational and entertainment value.

In almost all abuse stories, the husband suffers little or no retribution. In the story, "The Woman Who Got Stuck," a husband becomes violent when he learns of his wife's infidelty.

> A wealthy merchant who wanted to please his wife brought her a special gift, a goose that can be roasted, eaten and then comes to life again. The wife was delighted. The next day while the husband was at work, the wife entertained her lover and tried to roast the goose. The goose would not cooperate, and when the wife hit the goose, she became stuck to the goose. The woman's lover and anyone else who tried to pry them apart immediately became stuck together. Everyone in town came running to view this strange sight. When the husband saw them, the wife became very frightened and confessed the truth. That broke the spell, and the group became unstuck. The husband attacked the lover with a stick and then took his wife home and beat her badly.

The husband in this story saw himself as the final arbiter of his wife's behavior. His actions are presented as appropriate for a wronged man. The story confirms his right to determine and administer punishment. This view coincides with current research about batterers, as Demie Kurz observes:

> Interviews with batterers . . . show that men believe they are justified in their use of violence by their wives' behavior or by what they feel are accepted norms.[4]

Citing earlier laws and judicial decisions, Kurz points to the long history of societal support for and acceptance of a husband's right to use force to control his wife. Recognizing that laws have now changed to grant women more legal protection, she nevertheless finds that many police officers, judges, health professionals, etc., continue to believe that wife battering is a family affair.

Wife Beating Is Effective

The efficacy of wife-beating is demonstrated by the Shrew changing her disagreeable ways and becoming a docile and obedient Good Woman. As Bart pointed out regarding the American scene, "Physical force or the threat of violence are routinely employed [by men] if other means of control [of women] fail."[5] Folkstories support this conclusion, as illustrated in the story, "The Woman Who Loved Fairytales."

> An innkeeper's wife accepted only those lodgers who would tell her fairytales. The husband thought up a plan to cure her of this habit, which caused him financial losses. He hired an old peasant to come to the inn and offer to tell stories all night long. He then warned his wife not to interrupt the old man no matter what he said. The old peasant recited the same sentence over and over again until the perplexed wife finally asked why he kept saying the same thing. This was what the husband was waiting for. The husband seized his wife for interrupting and beat her so badly that from then on she hated stories and would no longer listen to them.

In this story, the husband planned a strategy to cure his wife's failing. Instead of trying to discuss with her a mutually acceptable solution, he tricked her into disobeying him. This gave him a justifiable excuse for beating her, and effectively getting what he wanted.

Men, Not Women, Act Irresponsibly

The lack of accountability regarding the Boss's actions in the stories reflects a pervasive social acceptance of male domination and of male irresponsibility. As stated by Kurz above, men who batter feel justified in using violence against their wives, and therefore do not feel accountable for this behavior. In folkstories, Bosses are shown in a less than mature stance, that of wanting their own way at any cost and not expecting to account for their actions in achieving it. "The Woman Who Worked Very Hard" portrays a man of this type.

> A hard-working wife was constantly after her lazy husband to help out with the work. They were very poor and needed everything they could make. Very tired one night, they began to quarrel about their terrible circumstances. Becoming increasingly hostile, the lazy husband threatened his wife with bodily harm. Incensed at his lack of ambition and his disregard for her welfare, she called him names and tried to hit him. But he grabbed her and pressed her head into the pillow. That ended the quarrel.

This husband acted irresponsibly throughout the story. He was not providing properly for the household. He resented having to work hard. He felt self-righteous and threatened her over disagreements. And when she finally became angry and aggressive, he had an excuse to destroy her. His actions are nowhere called into account.

Women, on the other hand, are usually held accountable for their actions. An example is the story, "The Woman Who Beat her Husband."

> An old woman constantly threw things at and beat her old husband. The long-suffering husband had no way of stopping her. One day to his surprise, he found two magic sacks: a good one containing sprites who prepared lavish meals and a bad one containing ogres who thrashed everyone. He was delighted; he now knew what to do. He brought the sacks home to his wife, and showed her only the good one. By his saying magic words, the sprites came out and covered the table with wonderful food; and the married pair enjoyed a good meal. Later, unbeknownst to his wife, he switched the sacks and urged his wife to perform the magic. She did, and the ogres came out and beat her mercilessly. After a while the husband, determining that the punishment was sufficient, proudly recited another magic chant to send the ogres back into the sack. The wife is now a good woman, and husband and wife live a contented life.

The difference between an abusive husband and an abusive wife is made clear: a wife is severely punished for attacking a husband, but a husband is not at fault for engineering an attack on his wife. On the contrary, he is rewarded.

Women Do Not Initiate Abusive Actions

The above story is unusual in showing a wife at first beating her husband. Very few such actions are part of marriage stories. In folkstories, women rarely physically abuse husbands. Wives may be disobedient or deceitful but very rarely violent. And they are generally not able to protect themselves against abusive spouses.

Recent newspaper accounts of physically aggressive wives show their actions to be largely self-protective, after long periods of severe inhuman treatment by their husbands. Like folkstory women, these wives are punished and often imprisoned for their violent acts.

Power, Not Anger, Motivates Wife Beating

A recent study by Pence and Paymar, bringing new insights to the causes of spouse abuse, found that "It is the desire for power that motivates men to become violent, and not uncontrollable anger as had been previously supposed."[6]

Again this finding is illustrated in folklore. A major issue in stories that end in violence is male power and control. Bosses are not uncontrollably angry. They are frustrated at having their will thwarted. "The Woman Who Was Jealous" reveals a battle for control.

> A woman in old China was proud, jealous, and strong, and as a result her husband was too afraid of her to take a second wife. Because the woman bore no children, her husband was given a concubine by the chancellor to provide him with children. The wife was infuriated and made life miserable for them all. The chancellor, through a series of carefully arranged circumstances, made sure the woman was beaten, humiliated, and terrorized to force her to comply with her husband's wishes. In the end, she was grateful to her husband for rescuing her, and she was willing to accept the new woman in the household.

In this story, the chancellor acted for the husband by forcing the wife to comply with male rule. He methodically planned a series of brutal situations to make the woman subservient to her husband.

According to Straus, Gellis and Steinmetz, "It often takes only one such event to fix the balance of power for many years—or perhaps for a lifetime."[7] This too is the message of the stories. By the end of most wife abuse stories, wives like the one above have permanently ceded control to the Boss.

There is No Typical Abusive Man

Abuse research has failed to find a profile of a typical abusive man. Men from all walks of life, degree of wealth, occupation, education, and racial background are liable to be wife batterers. The one common denominator is that they are all men. Similarly in the stories, poor peasants, wealthy merchants, beggars, kings, landowners, educated mandarins, war heroes, and many others from Russia, China, Italy, Vietnam, Germany, England, and elsewhere are Bosses and abusers of women. The common denominator here too is that they are all men. Men are shown to be physically and psychologically able to inflict damage on women with impunity. Women are generally physically and often psychologically unable to ward off attacks. The larger community, through ideological acquiescence and legal maneuvering, seems to support this state of affairs, both in life and in folkstories.

Physical Strength Differences Contribute to Wife Abuse

Scholarly discussions of wife abuse have centered on differences in female/male socialization processes, aggressive tendencies, hormonal balance, and desire for power and control as explanations of why men batter women. Physical size and strength difference as a factor in wife abuse has generally been side-stepped. But this theme does appear in the folkstories, and should be given some attention.

In the stories, physical violence is the ultimate controlling method used by men. Stories point to the fact that the generally greater physical strength of men contributes to their success in dominating women.

In scholarly literature, genetic strength differences have been explained in terms of prehistoric origins and of hormonal and environmental correlates. But the psychological effect of these differences on spouse relationships has not been explored.

Richard Leakey is one of the few who has even mentioned possible behavioral effects of this phenomenon. As cited in Roberta Hall's work on human size/strength differences, Leakey found a 20% average size differential between men and women. He is quoted as follows:

One may ponder on what this degree of human sexual dimorphism implies for the relationship between the sexes in the past—and in the present for that matter.[8]

The extent of strength differences is discussed by Anne Fausto-Sterling, in her study of the biology of men and women, as follows:

The average strength differences between men and women result at least in part from men's larger size. The upper body strength of the average female (that is, strength derived from arms and shoulders) is about half that of the average male . . . The lower body strength of the average woman reaches 70% of the average man's.[9]

Some feminists have been unhappy with a focus on physical strength in gender relations. The concern is that this trait and its effects seem to be relatively immutable, and thus discourage the hope of gender equality. A folkstory focusing directly on the subject gives them some support.

The story, "The Woman Who Used to be Strong," tells the following tale about how physical differences originated.

When God made the first man and woman, they were of equal strength, and they did the same things. Because of this equality, they were evenly matched, and neither could get the better of the other. The man was dissatisfied because he wanted to rule over the woman. He asked God about this, and God made him the stronger one. Then he announced to the woman that he was the Boss. He beat her up every time she disobeyed him. Distressed and very angry, the woman complained to God. God explained to her that once He gave something He could not take it back; and man would always be stronger than woman. Appealing to the Devil and acting on his advice, the woman then asked God for certain keys, which were granted her. According to the Devil, one was the key to the kitchen, another the key to the bedroom, and a third the key to the cradle. By using these keys wisely, the Devil said, the woman might be able to deal with man's greater strength. And that's the way it is.

As the story indicates, an awareness of the importance of strength differences has existed for a long time. The story implies further that man's greater strength is God-given, while women's wiles are inspired by the Devil. Spouses live daily with the effects of these differences, a subject that deserves greater attention from scholars and researchers.

An interesting contrast is contained in a letter of a young man seeking advice from Ann Landers. Citing the fact that his fiancee is so strong and athletic that, if she wished, she could make "mincemeat" out of him, he ponders:

> My fiancee is even-tempered and we get along well together . . . but just knowing she is physically stronger than I am makes me wonder if I should marry her.[10]

Strength inequality is seen as a problem when the man is physically weaker and the woman physically stronger. This man experienced the fear and recognized the danger of possible physical harm. The reverse is generally considered normal and proper: the man apparently should be the stronger one. Women rarely wonder out loud about the danger of marrying someone physically stronger than themselves, as the young man did. Yet battered, frightened, and threatened wives can attest to such danger, which they face daily as a normal situation.

An important question is what psychological outlooks have resulted from this physical difference. How have these outlooks been solidified into the cultural conditioning of women and men over the centuries and millenia? Some insight is available from recent research.

Work done by Mcarthur and Apathow[11] shows that people whose faces have a baby-like quality are perceived as subordinate and physically weak. These qualities are considered attractive in women, but unattractive in men. Such cultural conditioning in how we value strength and dominance can be dangerous in marital relations.

According to Richardson et al,[12] many men are taught not to assault women. However these inhibitions begin to disappear if women openly criticize them for performing badly on traditionally masculine tasks. Men were less likely to harm women who merely observed but were not openly critical. This finding supports the views of Straus[13] and of the folkstories, that men use physical force to demonstrate and protect their superiority and masculinity.

The stories repeatedly reveal this view. Wives are in greatest danger when being critical, carping, disobedient, nagging, ambitious, and generally challenging to man's dominance. Many otherwise peaceful men may then use their greater strength as a weapon and prevail in a physical attack. There are two basic rationales: a husband needs to appear dominant; and a physical attack is usually available, if needed, to impose and maintain this dominance.

Despite the widespread belief that men have always held a superior position in spouse relations, Marija Gimbutas,[14] among others, supports a contrary view. Based on archaeological evidence, she hypothesizes that women and men lived in peace and gender equality in prehistoric southern Europe. Notions of violence and male dominance were probably introduced by marauding groups at a later time. Despite the scholarly controversy stirred by these views, her work reflects a hope for creating or recreating a more humane and egalitarian structure in human society.

Alternative methods of gender relations, however, need to be developed for a better society in the future. From research on animal behavior we may glean some suggestive possibilities. For example, Wendy Jackson[15] showed that dominant-subordinate relations between animals can respond to environmental conditioning. From crayfish to monkeys, she found that animals who possess dominant characteristics (e.g., greater size, strength, and motivation) can be conditioned to adopt non-aggressive behavior. Granted that human beings are much more complex than animals, still this research raises interesting questions about equalizing marriage relationships. Much more needs to be known about the interplay of human physical and psychological traits to reeducate people for more wholesome marriage roles.

General Comments

Folkstories bear witness to the shameful widespread prevalence and banal acceptance of violence against women. The stories increase our understanding of domestic strife and provide evidence for the statement by Jane Caputi that ". . . wifehood . . .[is] an endemically unsafe occupation."[16] The folkstories clearly highlight the need for safer marriages for women and greater maturity and responsibility for men.

5
Love and Marriage

Marriage as an arena for conflicts, battles, and violence is a discouraging thought. The popular notion that love and marriage are linked is more comforting. Yet the high divorce rate, increasing domestic violence, and widespread infidelity all raise questions about how durable love is in the marriage relationship. A commentator on the modern scene recently remarked, "A lot of love is wasted before marriage that could be put to good use afterwards." The existence of so much dissension in the closest of human relationships is part of our inherited past and has continued into the present. Leslie's comments are instructive.

> Research has not yet provided final answers on the nature
> of love involvement before marriage. Neither has it indicated how functional or dysfunctional love is for subsequent
> marriage adjustment.[1]

Folklore has long recognized the contradiction between romantic expectations and the harsh realities of marriage. The following old folk sayings reveal such conflicting views.[2]

> Girl, do not exult in thy wedding dress; see
>   how much trouble lurks behind it.
> Husband and wife in perfect accord are like
>   the music of the harp and lute.
> If marriages are made in heaven, you have but
>   few friends there.
> Without a wife, the house is the abode of the
>   devil. With a wife, the house doth joy [sic].
> Marriage is the sunset of love.

And an old folk-rhyme:

When a couple are newly married,
The first month is honeymoon, or smick-smack,
The second is hither and thither,
The third is thwick-thwack,
The fourth, the devil take them that brought thee and I [sic]
    together.

While these sayings reveal long-time concerns over the desire for, but all too frequent lack of contentment in marriage, they contain little to explain or understand the situation. Many scholars have written about the romantic side of courtship, but not so many about love or the lack of it in marriage. According to Erich Fromm:

There is hardly any other activity, any enterprise, which is started with such tremendous hopes and expectations, and yet, which fails so regularly. . .If this were the case with any other activity, people would be eager to know the reasons for the failure and to learn how one could do better.[3]

An increasing number of psychologists and sociologists have been examining these difficult issues. Evidence from folkstories compared with recent scholarly writing helps explain the complex and confusing picture of love in marriage.

Love in Marriage

William Goode sees romantic love as important in facilitating mate selection and holding "a couple together long enough to allow them to begin marriage."[4] He stresses that love is found more in myth than in reality, and probably of more interest in the United States than elsewhere in the world.

Psychologist Frederick Meeker has been quoted as saying that romantic love has a short half-life and decays quickly like radioactive material. What remains for marriage partners is the need for acceptance and a dependence on one another for comfort, security, and self-esteem.[5] Thus threats to one's comfort, security or self-esteem can create major problems between spouses.

Joyce Brothers[6] calls attention to the use of exploitation in love relationships, one partner (generally the male) imposing a subordinate position on the other (usually the female).

According to Peter Pineo,[7] marital relationships in different families begin to resemble each other over time, regardless of the method of choice or the depth of love before marriage. Love, often important in selecting a mate, hardly remains a factor in solving critical problems afterward.

The texts of folkstories clearly reveal the paradox of the marriage institution. The problems of love in marriage seem all too familiar, even though today's sociocultural context differs from those of the stories. Incompatible folkstory couples tend to avoid probing the reasons for their difficulties or learning how to do better.

Courtship stories are replete with declarations of affectionate feelings, demonstrations of loyalty, and acts of bravery, all to impress and to win a favored choice of mate. These traits so important in courtship are hardly visible in marriage stories. In very few marriage stories is the word *love* even mentioned. Love is not presented as the underlying dynamic in most marriage stories. When mentioned, it is often tangential to the story.

Emotional relationships between folkstory spouses reveal inconsistent patterns. In Shrew/Boss stories, spouses tolerate each other in a combative way of life. Whatever feelings exist are far from the romantic love of courtship. For example, in the story, "The Woman Who Fooled Her Husband," the relationship between the spouses is one of antipathy rather than of love.

> An ingenious wife claimed to be ill when her husband was at home, but enjoyed herself whenever he was gone. She often sent her husband away to find medicine for her illnesses. One day he met a cousin who was concerned over the man's plight. The cousin offered to accompany him home and help cure the wife of her maladies. Upon reaching home, they discovered that the wife was merrily entertaining several men. Shocked, the husband did not know what to do. The cousin immediately made a suggestion. The husband then took a whip off the wall and attacked his wife mercilessly. Thereafter she no longer deceived him.

It is hard to believe that love was present in this marriage. Obviously the wife had already lost concern and affection for her husband. And a husband who chooses to solve this problem with such

brutality may be motivated by outrage, frustration, shame, or embarrassment, or he may just be following instructions. But he is hardly
motivated by love.

Stories about the Good Woman and the Boss contain elements of
love between the spouses. The Good Woman may be cherished by her
husband, if not in the beginning, then by the end of the story. Usually
after wives have suffered the hardships imposed by husbands, these
men finally appreciate their totally compliant women. In the relationship, the husband's self-concern and exploitation and the wife's depen-
dency do not seem grounded in love. An example is the story, "The
Woman Who Was Not Wise."

> Recognizing that his good but foolish wife tended to make
> poor decisions, a peasant warned her against trading any of
> their property while he was away. He threatened to beat her
> if she did anything stupid. Upon his return, he learned of the
> poor trade she had been talked into. Despite his threat, he
> felt sorry for her and restrained himself from beating her.
> He decided that if he found people more foolish than she, he
> would not beat her. He then went out and took advantage
> of several people, who made very poor trades with him.
> Satisfied, he returned home and spared his wife this time,
> saying, "I'll save it for next time."

This husband is shown as cruel and minimally caring. His wife
seems to live with constant threats of harm for her inability to function
normally. Although she is a Good Woman, she is offered very little love
by her husband.

Wise Woman/Puppet stories often end with the husband's
admiration of the woman. The Wise Woman is usually concerned about
her husband and family. And the beneficial results of her actions
usually inspire her husband's increased approval and affection. The
story, "The Woman Who Spared Her Husband" is an example.

> A famous rabbi returned to his home on the Sabbath and
> asked where his two sons were. His wife did not want to tell
> him before the Sabbath meal that his sons had died that
> morning. Therefore she told him the boys were still in the
> House of Study. After the Rabbi had something to eat and
> drink, she thought of a way to break the news gently. She

asked whether she should return some jewels that an owner had entrusted to her. The Rabbi assured her that was necessary. She then showed him the dead children, and stated that the Lord had given them and now had taken them away. Despite his deep grief, the rabbi thanked the Lord for his kind, wise, and virtuous wife.

In general, the Wise Wife is more concerned with her husband's welfare and self-esteem than he is with hers. Husbands accept the ministrations of their Wise Wives, but rarely reciprocate.

Obviously, love has different meanings in different marriages. The word may be the same, but the attitudes are not. Even in one individual, love can encompass a variety of feelings. The story, "The Woman Who Was Almost Killed," is a good illustration.

A farmer had a good and beautiful wife whom he loved deeply, and was therefore very jealous. When a stranger arrived in a storm asking for shelter, the farmer let him in, but soon became wary of the handsome newcomer. Self-conscious of his own looks, the husband thought the stranger and his wife made a very good-looking couple. Then he caught the stranger glancing at his wife, and decided that the two must be having an affair behind his back. When the stranger went to bed, the incensed husband took his wife out to kill her. After he had made several unsuccessful attempts to hang her from a tree, the dawn began to break. In the morning light, he realized his mistake and was contrite. He and his wife went home holding hands.

What is called love in this story was quickly translated into extreme jealousy, anger, and attempted murder. Love can have many meanings, and in this story it meant the following: pride (at having so beautiful a wife), insecurity (that his looks did not match his wife's), poor self-image (regarding his inadequacy compared with the visitor), jealousy (at the attentions of another man to his wife), shame (believing he did not retain his wife's affection), a threat to his masculinity (assuming his wife was unfaithful), and a reassertion of his masculinity (judging and punishing his wife). Nowhere is his love connected with any concern for his wife's welfare, dignity, personhood, or testimony.

The story shows that what is called *love* can easily go along with wife abuse, and can actually inspire it. When one realizes that the man was concerned about his own confused feelings and not his wife's welfare, his actions make more sense. Without trust, respect, discussion, clarification, and compromise, the word love seems misplaced. A different word is needed for the husband's self-indulgent feelings.

The Meaning of Love

Erich Fromm[8] has attempted to clarify and to sharpen the meaning of the word love. Instead of viewing love as something one falls into, he sees loving as an art to be learned and practiced throughout one's lifetime. Expecting love to happen and continue on its own leads to disappointment and failure. The active practice of loving, on the other hand, can endure in marriage and throughout one's life.

Fromm suggests four components of a mature enduring love: knowledge, respect, caring, and responsibility. *To love* means to know and understand another person very well; based on this knowledge, to respect who the other is, to care about the other's welfare, and to be willing and able to respond to the other's needs. Such love does not include sudden overwhelming feelings, exploition of another, a tool for establishing a marriage, or a self-centered concern with one's own needs.

In most folkstories, love as knowledge, respect, care, and responsibility is noticeably absent. Shrews and Bosses exhibit little mutual respect. Husbands of Good Women and of Wise Women are more concerned with themselves than with the welfare of their wives. Good Women do not seem to understand their husbands, and they are unable to respond suitably to a confusing situation. The Wise Woman is perhaps the only spouse who responds in her own way to what she believes the situation needs. However, mutual respect is missing as the woman manipulates the man to conform to her wishes.

On the other hand, folkstories of Assertive Spouses illustrate the art of loving. Unlike most other folkstory couples, these husbands and wives seem to know, care about and respect each other, and try to respond to each other's needs even at the risk of death.

The Essence of Marriage

The challenges of married life are many, and the presence or absence of mature love can make a big difference in a household. A framework for looking at marriage has been provided by Niklas Luhmann[9]. In his exhaustive study of love and marriage over several centuries, he sums up the essence of marriage, as follows:

Marriage is not expected to provide one with a completely unrealistic ideal world and definitely not a perpetual affirmation of passionate feelings, but rather with a basis for communication and common action with regard to everything which is of importance to the partners involved.[10]

Thus marriage is seen as an arena for sharing information and acting together on matters of importance. Folkstory marriage tends to fall far short of this ideal.

Communication Patterns

Luhmann expects shared communication to be an integral part of marriage. Yet folkstories indicate the difficulty and often reluctance spouses have in sharing views with each other.

Most folkstory marriage partners communicate poorly. Husbands wish to withhold information from their wives, nurse grievances, talk harshly, and force their wives into submission. Wives, on the other hand, are more talkative, less violent, and often circumspect. They may nag, wheedle, manipulate through deception, or remain totally silent; and they are often regarded as Shrews when they communicate directly and openly.

Instead of a basis for exchanging information, marriage becomes for many an arena for misunderstanding. Thus love based on knowledge and understanding, as Fromm suggests, becomes impossible, and a marriage based on good communication cannot exist.

Men's practice of withholding information is strengthened in some stories by a god or spirit warning the husband that the punishment for telling the truth is death. The cultural message is that a wife is not entitled to an explanation of her husband's behavior. Through being punished or threatened, wives learn to avoid asking about things they do not understand.

Harsh, arrogant husbands are found in many stories, for example, "The Woman Who Displeased her Husband."

A mean old man was married to a good and hard-working woman. But he was never satisfied. He beat the woman so badly that the magistrate ordered him to appear in court. The verdict was that he must not beat his wife any more, but instead must share joys and sorrows with her, as is appropriate in marriage. He complied by not beating her; instead he threw things at her. Back in the courtroom again, he protested that he had carried out the court order. Not only was he no longer beating his wife, but he also was sharing joys and sorrows. When something hit her, he was joyous and she sorrowful; when he missed, she was joyous and he sorrowful. The magistrate had to think of another punishment for him.

This story differs from other stories of batterers in that this husband was held accountable for his cruelty. His testimony revealed him as a callous brute whose idea of communication compounded the tragedy of the marriage. The story, however, seems to be told as a joke—the man's logic, comical; the woman's plight, unimportant.

Among wives, the Shrew is shown typically as a nag and a scold. These women use communication as a constant irritant, keeping after their husbands with incessant demands until the husbands' resistance is broken down. This theme is openly shown in the story, "The Woman Who Persisted."

A nagging wife wheedled answers and agreements from her unwilling husband. The husband tried to refuse his wife, but her persistence and sweet talk overcame his resistance. In resignation, he told her everything she wanted to know.

Many Good Women communicate with their husbands in ways that suit the men completely. These women are supportive, encouraging, respectful, adoring, and compliant. They maintain these qualities even when they are treated badly by their husbands. Their compliant communication may well mask what they feel. It is hard to believe that wives are content when they are reticent about mistreatment. An example is the wife in the story, "The Woman Who Pulled the Wagon." This woman is first shown in a negative light and then as a Good Woman. In neither capacity does she communicate her feelings.

A gruff lonely man asked to marry the *barin*'s [local nobleman] daughter. The *barin* agreed, but warned him of the woman's capriciousness. After marriage, the husband decided to solve that problem. Pretending to be drunk, he became violent and scared his wife badly. Some time later on the way to visit her family, he continued to abuse her by harnessing her to their wagon and making her pull it. When they arrived, her father, the *barin*, thanked the husband for showing how to deal with shrews. Thereafter the woman became obedient and compliant.

In this story, the wife communicates nothing of her feelings. Open communication is non-existent between the spouses, and actions are mainly hostile rather than caring.

For Wise Women, deception is a standard form of communication. Often this is the only way a wife can communicate with her husband and get her views accepted. The story, "The Woman Who Was Sent Away," is an example.

A prince married an unusually beautiful but poor young woman. He later learned that a nobleman was making advances toward his wife, which he thought were reciprocated. Without investigating further, he ordered her exiled. A ship took her to a foreign port and left her there. After changing her identity to a male, she eventually returned home, and through disguise, masquerade, and many deceptions, arranged for her husband to recognize her innocence. The wife and husband were reunited in happiness.

As illustrated in this story, Wise Women for the most part do not confide in their husbands, but tell them only enough to achieve their aims.

Different from these spouses, Assertive Women and Men approximate Luhmann's idea of communication as an important asset in marriage. They are able to express in words and actions genuine concern for each other. Their communication tends to be open and clear. Assertive Wives deal with their husbands directly and honestly without fear of violence or antagonism. These few couples participate in self-respecting shared relationships. They conform more closely to the cultural ideals of caring and sharing in marriage. In the story, "The Woman Who Did Not Like Boasting," the wife is forthright and open in her criticism of her husband. She is proven right in the end and suffers no harm for her direct approach.

There was a conceited man who always boasted of his importance, to his wife's great dissatisfaction. She warned him that he would be in trouble if he ever met a strong competitor. The test came when the wife told her husband she had discovered a giant. Her husband insisted on going to meet and challenge this giant. Reluctantly the woman revealed where the giant lived. Despite his bravado, when the husband found the giant, he was terrified and had to flee. The chastened husband returned home to his wife, who reminded him once again that there is always someone better than oneself, and idle boasting is unbecoming.

In general, Good Women tell husbands in a pleasant way what the men want to hear. Shrews tell husbands in a direct manner what the men do not want to hear. Wise Women tell their husbands only what will advance the wife's goals. Assertive Women, on the other hand, state their ideas clearly and are heard with care and concern by their husbands.

Judged according to Fromm's and Luhmann's formulations, communication between most spouses leaves much to be desired. Communication in folkstory marriage is more often a problem than an aid. Goals are self-serving, as spouses concentrate on their own needs with little attention to those of their spouses. Except for Assertive Wives and Husbands, most folkstory couples share little that would encourage mutual understanding; good communication, as Luhmann suggests, and love in Fromm's terms tend to be absent.

Common Action

Folkstories repeatedly illustrate that each partner in a marriage is vitally affected by the actions of the other. Spouses are, therefore, very concerned about what the other does. Recognizing this great interdependence, marriage partners are always trying to influence the behavior of their mates. Each tries to create and maintain the kind of life that suits her/himself best.

Folkstory spouses face all kinds of situations together. While dealing with the same external circumstances, however, they each tend to act independently of each other. Mutually arrived at decisions for common action are not the rule. For example, in Good Woman/Boss and Shrew/Tolerant Man stories, one spouse commands the other with no possibility of shared discussion or agreement. In many stories, force is used to compel compliance. Wise Women always act unilaterally.

Scanzoni and Scinovacz in their study of modern family life call marriages where the woman is compliant (e.g., Good Woman) and the man is dominant (e.g., Boss) *the traditional relationship.* In such marriages, these scholars claim that decision making becomes superfluous, and action predictable. They quote Spiegel as saying, "The person knows his [sic] parts so well . . . he enacts them automatically, and all goes well."[11] Folkstory scenes seem to contradict these views. Traditional marriages can take several different forms other than the Good Woman/Boss relationship. And stories about Shrews and Wise Women raise serious question about traditional women automatically fulfilling compliant and subservient roles.

In addition, many stories deal with couples changing their established behavior patterns. In stories about change, one spouse becomes increasingly unhappy about the actions of the other, and chooses to do something about it. The story, "The Woman Who Threatened to Leave," is an example.

> A woman watched her self-satisfied coachman husband drive the carriage of his employer, the Prime Minister. Upon arriving home one day, the coachman learned that his wife planned to leave him. In response to his questioning, she explained that the Prime Minister, despite his important position, was a humble man; whereas her husband, only a coachman, put on arrogant airs. The chastened coachman reconsidered his behavior and became more modest. The Prime Minister, noting the change, rewarded the coachman with a better position.

Wise Women stories like this one involve a wife's action in changing her husband's behavior, generally by manipulating the situation without direct confrontation.

In most stories, techniques for changing a spouse's behavior are female manipulation and male violence. Mutual agreement on actions is hard to find, except in some stories of Assertive Spouses. The story, "The Woman Couldn't Explain," told earlier (p. 20), illustrates the harm that can result to Assertive Spouses if one goes back on an agreed upon action.

Items of Importance

Marriage partners generally agree on areas of importance in marriage. Appearing repeatedly in folkstory conflicts are four major concerns: family finances, infidelity, proper behavior, and status. Even small inconsequential actions in any one of these areas may be perceived as a threat by a spouse.

The story, "The Woman Who Was a Gossip," is a good example.

> An old man was angry because his wife told people about a
> secret treasure they had found. To teach her a lesson, he
> fooled her into thinking strange things were happening.
> When they were summoned by the mayor, who wanted to
> know more about the treasure, the husband accused his wife
> of lying. To prove his point, he asked her to recount the
> strange events he had made her believe. The mayor was
> then convinced that the woman was a liar, ordered her
> thrashed for lying, and sent them home.

In this story, family finances, proper behavior and status were all
involved in the conflict between the spouses. The husband was concerned about preserving his new-found wealth and improving his wife's
behavior. On the other hand, by revealing their treasure, the wife wished
to enhance their status in the eyes of the community.

The story, "The Woman Who Thought She Was a Widow," reveals
a husband's inordinate concern over fidelity.

> In order to test his wife's faithfulness, a man with small
> beady eyes pretended to be dead. Soon suitors began to
> court his wife. Consumed with grief, she sent all the suitors
> away until finally one arrived with small beady eyes just
> like her late husband. Delighted, she ordered her husband's
> body removed; and she and the newcomer planned to be
> married. When the wedding began, her old husband rushed
> in and beat everyone badly, including his wife.

General Conclusions

Compared with the Luhmann formulation that marriage is "a
basis for communication and common action with regard to everything
which is of importance to the partners involved," we find that folkstories give a different view. While marriage partners may agree on
which areas of life are important, there is little consensus on specific
action to be pursued in these important areas. And marriage as a basis
for good communication leaves much to be desired.

Two main obstacles to peace and harmony in marriage appear to
be: 1) the desire of each spouse to win in conflicts, and 2) the requirement that the husband rule the household. The search for the best

solution to common problems, the use of open and direct discussion for handling situations, and objective evaluation of ways to proceed in new circumstances are sacrificed to these ends.

The stories are noticeably lacking in mutuality, intimacy, equality, negotiation, or compromise. The necessary interdependence of the marriage relationship leads instead to uncertainty, suspicion, distrust, and aggression. The nature of love and marriage in most stories shows the need for vast improvements in how people relate to each other, communicate, and work together on common problems.

The Difference Between Love and War

In recent years, feminist writers have questioned the possibility of happiness in marriages based on fighting to win, and on dominance and compliance. Although most folkstory marriages seem bereft of good relationships, a few give the impression that love and happiness are compatible with domination, brutality, subservience or trickery. To many scholars, however, this idea is misleading and dangerous.[12]

For example, Carolyn Heilbrun states, "Male domination produces men incapable of loving, and women incapable of self-hood."[13] Miriam Johnson states that given the requirement of male dominance, "men become less human, and women do too."[14]

Harris and McNamara write:

> Women frequently find themselves in the painful position of trying to conform to life-cycle patterns and roles that do not reflect their own talents and inclinations. . . Male control . . . distorts female behavior and attitudes.[15]

Questions arise as to whether the battle-of-the-sexes is a natural phenomenon over which we have little control. Recent research finds otherwise. Tikva Frymer-Kensky, writing about gender roles in biblical times, states:

> The difference in activity between women and men is circumstantial rather than innate; both use the powers and strategies of the world in which they find themselves.[16]

Gloria Steinem confronts the issue as follows:

> On the one hand, each of us is born with a full circle of human qualities . . . On the other hand, societies ask us to play totalitarian gender roles that . . . assign behavior . .

and are so accepted that they may be seen as part of nature. Societies have been . . . intent on creating differences where none exists.[17]

But not all societies require hierarchical exploitative gender roles. The stories of Assertive Spouses demonstrate greater equality between women and men, and a better environment for love to flourish.

Recent writers have also found a connection between equality and love. Vannoy-Hiller and Philliber studied the effect on modern marriages of wives who have independent successful careers. Among their findings are the following:

> The simple conclusion . . . is that one partner's need to be better than his or her spouse is incompatible with the emotional bonds that produce a high-quality marriage.

Their single most important finding about gender-role is:

> the pervasive importance of a husband's sensitivity . . . a husband with a supportive personality, sensitive to his wife's feelings, is critical in a high-quality marriage.[18]

Gloria Steinem lends support to these findings in her perception of love.

> Love is not about power . . . If we love someone . . . we can't own, absorb, or change them. We can only help them become what they already are . . . *When we argue with someone we love, for instance, it's more about trying to make ourselves understood than trying to win*[19] [Italics added].

These comments help explain the difference between love and war in the folkstories. Marriage-as-war stories occur against the background of patriarchal rule with abuse and violence as forms of control. The search for love in these marriages is seriously impaired by culturally prescribed gender roles.

In stories of Assertive Spouses, winning and male dominance are not prized. Without these constraints, husbands and wives are more easily able to behave with mutual respect and with self-respect. And the lack of competitiveness opens the way to good communication, joint decision making, and emotional satisfaction.

The fact that folkstories show such contrasts in behavior supports the idea that gender relationships are not innate. The question arises whether it is possible for spouses to act assertively in societies in which winning and male dominance remain strong cultural expectations. With so much current rhetoric on equality in marriage, is it possible for spouses to deviate from the behavioral norm of inequality and strife?

This is not an easy task, as Vannoy-Hiller and Philliber recognize:

> It is a challenge to worry less about conforming consistently to gender-role prescriptions and simply to be oneself at the moment. . .In general, we do not look kindly on those who choose their own way.[20]

Difficult as this is, Steinem recommends the effort. "However great the struggle, the rewards are even greater."[21]

That personal changes can be achieved is revealed in the research of Stinnett and DeFrain.[22] They studied a large number of *strong families* in America. They found that, even in unsupportive cultural environments, many spouses found ways to develop wholesome patterns of communication, commitment, equality, respect, caring and assertiveness. To overcome entrenched personal and cultural attitudes and to effect new behavior patterns were extremely difficult tasks for these families. In the end, however, they were greatly rewarded for their efforts. The stories of strong families read like those of storybook Assertive Spouses.

6

Gender Roles in Different Cultures

An interesting aspect of marriage stories is the relative similarity of gender roles in many parts of the world. The finding is not unique.[1] Marriage relationships in different cultures often resemble each other.[2] Against this background of similarities, however, some cultural variation exists. Marriage stories portray both the similarities and differences.

Most folkstories published in the United States are identified as coming from different parts of the world (e.g., British folkstories, African folkstories). Editors of these works generally emphasize a desire and effort to preserve the cultural atmosphere of the stories. As a result, although texts can change with retelling,[3] these culturally defined tales tend to retain their unique world view.[4]

Stories from Three Major Culture Areas

In three major areas of the world, Europe, East Asia, and sub-Saharan Africa, folkstory gender roles reflect their culture of origin. In both Europe and East Asia, male dominance is of great importance. Husbands are likely to be the Boss, or to change into the Boss by the end of the story. Wives accommodate to these men in somewhat different ways. In European stories, direct confrontation by wives is all but intolerable. To survive, women must be either compliant or devious. Some East Asian stories portray similar patterns. In others, wives may prevail even when directly confronting and challenging male rule, a situation much less likely in European stories. Gender roles in African stories differ markedly from the other areas; African spouses tend to be assertive and more egalitarian in their relationship. Nevertheless there exist indications of male supremacy in some stories, and even an occasional story of wife abuse. Both these qualities are much less prevalent in African stories than in those from the other parts of the world.

European Stories

European stories tend toward Good Woman/Boss marriages. In some stories, wives are Good Women from the beginning; in others the wife starts out as a Shrew and is transformed into a Good Woman. This emphasis on compliance seems to be part of the European historical and cultural heritage.

Anderson and Zinsser summarize the findings of current research into women's history as follows:

> . . .gender has been the most important factor in
> shaping the lives of European women.
> . . .all European women. . .were subject to. . .European cul-
> ture's largely negative views of women.
> Considered innately flawed, less valuable, and thus inferior
> to men, all women were supposed to be subordinate to men.[5]

These views still echo in currently published European tales. Despite revisions from repeated retellings, the stories retain the negative and subordinate views of women.

Interesting regional differences exist, however, in how the wife reacts. Wives in Russian stories tend to be confrontational and aggressive (Shrews) and those in British stories, docile and compliant (Good Women).

In Russian stories, women are abused and usually forced to change into compliant Good Women. Many plots exemplify the Russian proverb, "A hen is not a bird, and a woman is not a person." The prevalence of wife beating in Russian folkstories is reflective of earlier Russian history when a woman was totally subject to her husband's authority. She was often required to live in segregated quarters and could be sold into slavery if her husband was in debt.[6] Many women rebelled under such harsh conditions.

A fairly typical Russian story is "The Woman Who Made Her Husband Miserable."

> A peasant had a wife he could not control. Whatever he
> tried to do, she disobeyed him and made him miserable.

Finally no longer able to tolerate her, he pushed her into a deep pit. For a few days he was happy. Then he became lonely and went to find his wife. When he lowered a rope into the pit for her, to his great surprise a gnome came up instead. The gnome was distraught over his few days with the difficult woman, and begged the husband to protect him. In exchange he offered to make the man very rich. The husband agreed. The gnome kept his word, and the husband became a wealthy man. No longer needing the gnome, the man tricked him into falling into the pit again. The man then married a beautiful young woman, while his old wife spent the rest of her days in the pit with the gnome.

In modern times, despite extensive communist rhetoric about gender equality, life continued to be harsh for women in Soviet[7] and post-Soviet regimes. Discrimination has been prevalent in employment even though over 90% of the female population works full-time. Women carry a crushing double burden of full-time work and full-time household responsiblities with little help from their husbands or the government. In some rural areas such practices as female slave markets, private wife exchanges, and wife murders may still persist.[8]

Many British stories on the other hand show wives mainly as Good Women married to the Boss. These women suffer ill-treatment without complaint. Only a few British folkstory wives are Shrews or Wise Women.

The compliant attitude of women has been noted in British history. According to Anderson and Zinsser:

> The majority of [British] peasant women throughout the centuries accepted the circumstances, the attitudes, and the necessities of survival even though they were left vulnerable and subordinate.[9]

The story, "The Woman Who Was Sold," shows a woman's quiet response to ill-treatment by her husband.

A poor tailor was very cruel to his good wife. Not wanting her any longer, he decided to offer her for sale. She willingly agreed. He put a rope around her neck and walked with her through the town. At first the townspeople saw this as a big joke. But then a decent old man bid for her. When they got to his house, she rewarded him with money she had hidden in her stocking. Thereafter the old man took good care of her. Her husband meanwhile was ridiculed as a cuckold by the townspeople.

In this story, the wife's only reaction to extreme violence was her willingness to be sold. Neither she nor the townspeople spoke out against a hateful brute. The townspeople even saw the husband's brutality and the wife's submissiveness as humorous.

Amanda Sebestyen notes that denial and reticence continue today as typical British ways of dealing with unpleasantness. She states, "English patriarchy has a hooded face; fewer street rapes, more wife-beating behind locked doors." She decries the continuing compliance of women and their reluctance to express anger at being abused.[10]

Summarizing European gender relations, Anderson and Zinsser point out that "negative cultural traditions [toward women] have proved the most powerful and the most resistant to change." And "no woman could escape the impact of these views completely."[11]

East Asian Stories

Wives in East Asian stories may be Good Women, Wise Women or Shrews. As in European stories, male dominance is expected in the Asian stories. Asian women are somewhat different from those in European stories. Contradictions in historic attitudes toward women in the East Asian heritage may provide some explanation.

Throughout Chinese history, there has always been a small minority of women in important political, literary, and community positions. In addition, there is a long tradition of Chinese women warriors, going back to the Tang dynasty and continuing into the Communist Revolution of modern times. On the other hand, women were severely restricted by the Confucian doctrine promulgated in the 5th century BC. Women were expected to obey their fathers, husbands, and sons, and to be silent, clean, humble, and hard-working.[12] Elsewhere in East Asia, for example in Vietnam, women tended to have higher status than in the Chinese patriarchy. The extension of Confucianism, however, brought along with it harsher attitudes toward women.

Although in Asian stories the husband tends to be the Boss, wives often act with resolution and purpose even when forced into submission. An example is "The Woman Who Broke an Egg."

A very poor farmer found an egg and imagined that this egg would bring him and his wife a fortune. He saw the egg hatching into a chicken. Then there would be many more eggs and many more chickens, which they would sell at great advantage. His wife went along with the fantasy until he mentioned that with that wealth, he could afford another wife. Enraged at this idea, she smashed the egg. The husband beat her and took her to the magistrate for further punishment. She was ordered to be killed for destroying their fortune.

She immediately protested that the wealth was not real, only a future idea. Her husband pointed out that the second wife was also a future idea. Appealing to the magistrate directly, the wife stressed that it was never too soon to prevent disaster. Won over, the magistrate released her and sent them both home.

The wife in this story overcame the magistrate's efforts to destroy her. Despite being beaten by her husband, she was not ultimately forced to accede to his wishes. On the other hand, the husband's right to abuse his wife is in no way challenged. In European stories, she would more likely be forced into submission by abuse or self-imposed compliance. The Asian story combines two cultural expectations: male dominance and self-reliant women.

Sub-Saharan African Stories

Sub-Saharan Africa is a very large land area with hundreds of different cultural groups that defy facile generalization. Nevertheless, lifestyle differences exist alongside modal cultural traits found in the area. These modal traits are reflected in many African stories.

An Assertive Husband and an Assertive Wife in a more or less egalitarian relationship are often found in African folkstories. Most stories tend to avoid patriarchal male-dominant themes. Violence is relatively rare. Conflicts are often resolved without harshness.

Historically, African wives as described in many anthropological studies differ markedly from wives in Europe or Asia. Sudarkasa states:

> Marriage in Africa was a contractual union which often involved long-lasting companionate relationships . . . . Interpersonal relationships within African families were

governed by . . . respect, restraint, responsibility, and reciprocity.[13]

Okonjo[14] enumerates the long established major roles of Nigerian women in farming, trading, and craft activities, often as the main bread-winners in the family, and frequently as significant participants in polit-ical decision making. Bohannan concludes that "Women in Africa are not, in short, a deprived group as they were in the nineteenth-century Western world."[15]

Levinson[16] reports that domestic violence has been present in varying degrees in African societies. However, even in societies where male dominance is culturally prescribed and wife beating common, mechanisms exist to mitigate serious harm. For example, a violent hus-band is often publicly humiliated by gossip in the marketplace; easy access to divorce is often used by women to escape from a battering husband; and women can return to their own families for protection.

Violence against a wife, though rare, sometimes appears in an African story. An example is "The Woman Who Was a Lioness."

In a time of great famine, the lions were very hungry. In order to get food for her starving cubs, one of the lionesses offered to change into a beautiful woman, marry and then kill a man who owned many head of cattle, and bring the cattle back for her cubs and the other lions.

Although she carried out part of her plan, her efforts to kill the man were thwarted by the man's son. One night, the son roused his father saying there was a wild animal in the house. When the father looked into the dark, he observed his wife changing into a lioness. He immediately took his son and left for the village. When he told the townspeople of the danger, they came and set fire to the house. The woman-lioness burned to death.

The story reveals the competition for scarce resources between people and animals during times of famine, a situation not uncommon in sub-Saharan Africa. Thus the woman had reason to act as she did; she is not cast as a nasty person, only a danger. The woman is recognized as having her own agenda, different from her husband's. In this case, the conflict was a serious threat to the survival of the community and force was used to prevent disaster. In other African stories, however, in which problems are couple-centered, the women's independence is more likely to be preserved, and conflicts resolved with mutual respect.

Stories from Marginal Populations

Two groups of stories from peoples who have been outside mainstream cultures reflect the influence of prejudice and discrimination. Experiences of deprivation, however, do not necessarily affect peoples in the same way. A comparison of African American stories and Jewish stories reveals that unique historical experiences can influence relationships in different ways.

In both sets of stories, wives are strong and independent. The roles of husbands are different. In African American stories, the man tends to be the Boss who uses violence to control the woman. Husbands in Jewish stories, on the other hand, are more likely to be Puppets or Tolerant Men; only rarely is a husband the Boss.

African American Stories

African American stories were influenced by both the African and the European heritages. The wife in most stories tends to appear as a strong, independent woman, continuing in large part the tradition of her African counterpart. Unlike the African woman, however, the African American woman is cast as an unpleasant Shrew similar to the European wife. The husband is the Boss, like most European story husbands. There tend to be few, if any, Good Women and/or Wise Women. Neither are there many Puppets or Tolerant Men.

An example is the story, "The Woman Who Did Not Understand."[17]

A great hunter successfully hunted many bush cows. To protect the rest of the herd, one of the cows transformed herself into a beautiful woman to lure the hunter back to the forest and kill him. She married the hunter for this purpose, and every night asked him for the secret of his success in hunting. The man explained that he could transform himself into many different forms to escape detection. But he fooled his wife by saying his last transformation was into a "nadanada," which means "nothing." His wife did not understand the word, but she lured him back to the forest. Changing into a bush cow, she told all the animals that his final transformation would be into a "nadanada." This confused them greatly, and they did not know what to do. Their confusion gave the hunter a chance to destroy most of the bush cows. He spared one—the pregnant cow, who had been his wife. But he tore her arm off and left her in the forest.

A complex of cultural factors influenced African American folkstories. Slavery created great physical and psychological trauma. Continuing into the post-slavery era, men were deprived of the usual indicators of masculine status: financial success, land or capital ownership, political power. Anger, hatred, and frustration often translated into violent outbursts.[18] According to Bernard,[19] in the African American community these outbursts would frequently be directed by men against women.

The dominant European culture fostered male supremacy and female subordination in the home. These ideas were reinforced by Church teachings, which became a major influence in African American life.[20]

Given the drastic effects of American slavery plus the influence of European cultural and religious teachings on family relationships, it is not surprising that African American folktales became replete with hostility, male dominance and violence against strong independent women.[21]

Jewish Stories

Jewish stories, created over centuries of discriminatory treatment and ghettoization, developed in a different way. In Jewish stories, independent wives are often seen as Shrews or Wise Women. The compliant Good Woman is rarely present in Jewish stories. Jewish men on the other hand tend to be manipulated Puppets or Tolerant Men. Few, if any, Jewish folktale husbands are the Boss.

An example is the story "The Woman Who Helped Her Husband."

A young, inept rabbi wanted a good post and let his wife do the negotiating for it. She succeeded, and he took over a fine congregation. In his new position, he became arrogant and boastful. His wife put him in his place by saying that he became a successful rabbi because of her, and not vice versa.

Given the fact that the Jewish people lived in and were influenced by many European and Near Eastern cultures in which patriarchal values prevailed, and that the Jewish heritage contains its own share of patriarchal teachings, these folktale images of strong women and non-controlling men need further explanation.

The Jewish people, forced into exile by the Roman conquest of Jerusalem in the first century A.D., became an uprooted and wandering population. Their history was one of settlement, expulsion, and resettlement, over two thousand years. Often without land or citizenship rights, they became largely an urban population of artisans and traders, remaining loyal to their religious faith, and dedicated to worship and study.[22]

Without the usual patriarchal symbols of male status—land ownership, military prowess, political power—Jewish men saw the essence of their masculinity in their achievements in the house of study and of worship.[23] As traders, many traveled widely, often leaving their wives to care for both home and business.[24] Over the centuries, many Jewish wives were active both in the home and in the working world. In addition, women had to be ready to pack and move, unpack and resettle, if conditions became untenable for the family where they were. Many religious men preferred to leave the details of daily life to their wives while they devoted themselves to spiritual matters, an activity considered more lofty and more desirable.

In the folkstories, we usually find the wife as the one who runs things and who often tells her husband what to do; and the husband, as a Tolerant Man or a Puppet, is accepting though not always satisfied with the resulting situation. Patriarchal attitudes may cast the active wife negatively, but the realities of living forced the husband generally to adjust to the situation.[25]

One Story in Three Cultures

In surveying folklore research, Alan Dundes states that folktales are not necessarily unique to only one cultural context. He points out that the same story often occurs in different locations and at different times.

The same story, however, is not told in exactly the same way in different cultures. Stories that are incorporated into the lore of different peoples tend to show distinctive cultural influences.[26] An illustration is a story belonging to three different cultural heritages—Italian, Jewish, and West African. Two of these three versions were recounted in earlier chapters.

The plot in each case is essentially the same: a husband learned to understand the language of animals, but he must not reveal this gift to anyone or he would die. The wife became suspicious and curious when the husband laughed at inappropriate times. In each case, when the man refused to explain what he was laughing at, the wife became upset and insistent.

The problem is roughly similar in all three stories. Cultural differences appear as each husband resolves his dilemma. The Italian husband is taught by a rooster to beat his wife into submission. He does this and she becomes a docile Good Woman. The Jewish husband does not attack his wife, but he does threaten her. This is sufficient for the woman to desist from further curiosity. The African husband, confronted by the dilemma of destroying his wife's confidence in him or losing his life, chooses to tell her the truth, and he dies.

The Italian husband follows a standard European folkstory pattern of changing the Shrew into a Good Woman through physical violence. The Jewish husband is one of the few Boss figures in Jewish folkstories, but he stops short of physically beating his wife. The African husband places his respect and concern for his wife above life itself.

Cultural Effects on Stories

According to Bascom,[27] folklore provides a cultural mirror by illustrating actions deemed proper within a particular group. As indicated above, folkstories from many parts of the world reveal that when patriarchal attitudes prevail in the home, women resort to specific adaptive roles. These cultural traits are then seen as models of past and future behavior.

Where the man must be the Boss, the woman can fight against his rule (the Shrew), adjust to and comply with his domination (the Good Woman), or circumvent his power (the Wise Woman). Which of these accommodations to the Boss is most prevalent in a particular society depends in part on its unique cultural history. In cultures more inclined to gender equality in which patriarchal attitudes are weaker or lacking, roles for wives and husbands involve greater mutuality, respect, and cooperation.

Marginal peoples, discriminated against by mainstream populations, develop gender roles in accordance with their unique cultural history. In both African American and Jewish stories, women are shown as strong independent people. The behavior of the husbands, on the other hand, reflects differences in male roles under differing conditions of status deprivation.

In different locations, the same story tends to conform to prevailing cultural traditions. Such adaptations are also found within the same geographic location but at different historical and cultural periods.

Changing Cultural Influences on Story Interpretation

Zipes has discussed at some length how, at different times in history, story texts were changed to conform to prevailing cultural outlooks. For example, stories circulating in the Middle Ages that stressed themes of maturation and integration were, at the beginning of the industrial era, "recast to stress domination and wealth."[28] Eighteenth and nineteenth century European folktale writers (e.g., Perrault and the Grimm Brothers, among others) revised the tales to advance the values of the emerging bourgeoisie. During the Nazi era in Germany, folktales were used to reinforce fascist ideology, not so much by changing the texts as by reinterpreting well-known stories. After the defeat of the Nazis, a concerted effort was made in Germany to counteract this invidious use of folkstories. More recently in the United States, in response to concerns over equal rights for women, collections of stories have appeared in which girls and women are active protagonists and heroines.[29]

In view of the long history of change in both story texts and story interpretations, one can look at marriage stories and consider how they might be interpreted in the future to advance the cause of better marriages.

Radner and Lanser[30] illustrate that women and men can read the same text and find different meanings in it. They indicate that appropriating stories from a male interpretation to a female one can provide interesting new insights. Given the fact that a great many currently published texts serve to justify male dominance in the home, it is instructive to reverse the focus and consider what a female view, or at least a more egalitarian view, would be.

In the story, "The Woman Who Was Stubborn," told in an earlier chapter (p. 8), a husband drowns his wife because she does not agree with him over the use of a particular word. The husband's actions illustrate that it is unacceptable for a wife to defy her husband; it is, however, acceptable for a husband to murder his wife, for which act he is not held accountable. The story offers a male view of appropriate behavior.

The characterizations of the wife as Shrew and the husband as Boss are implicit in the way this story appears in the literature. The story itself contains actions, but no labels. Only the title of the story indicates who the stubborn one is.

Reconsidering the story from a reverse vantage point can change the analysis. Were the story called "The Man Who Was Stubborn," the wife is no longer a Shrew, but a reasonable, intelligent human being expressing openly and directly an opinion different from her husband's. Her husband can then be seen as a stubborn ignoramus, who does not know the difference in meaning between two simple words. Instead of the story's supporting an ordinary husband who drowns a defiant wife, it would uncover the brutality and stupidity of a dangerous man against a sensible, strong-minded woman.

On the other hand, were the story called, "The Stubborn Couple," probably the most accurate designation of the action, we see two people unskilled at conflict resolution, understanding, and mutual respect. Using a single moral standard for both spouses, the husband's crime would require punishment. And the story would show that marriage is destroyed by stubbornness, mutual disrespect, and cruelty.

The story's present emphasis on male supremacy is clear. Given the horror of wife abuse, folkstories teaching the acceptability of wife-murder are dangerous and intolerable.

Another example of appropriation to a female viewpoint is the story, "The Woman Who Accepted Everything."

> A farmer and his wife were devoted to each other. She was totally accepting and approved of anything he did. To improve their circumstances, the wife suggested he take their cow to market to trade. Not concerned about the trading, the man made a series of bad errors, and came home with no cow and with nothing in exchange. He then made a bet with his neighbor that his wife would approve of his actions. He was right. She justified everything he did and was delighted to see him. The astonished neighbor had to pay the wager. The farmer and his wife thus made money that day, and continued to live happily.

From a male dominance point of view, the story shows the ideal female, one who accepts even the strangest behavior on the part of her husband. Both are rewarded for the wife's compliance by the money won from the neighbor.

Another way of looking at the same material is to see the wife as very tolerant of a seriously deficient husband. Read from a reverse point of view, the story reveals two flawed characters: a self-indulgent husband who basks in his dominant status, and a woman who abandons all good sense to avoid criticizing her husband. In an era of increasing educational and occupational opportunities for women, stories that glorify women of inane judgment and who are totally lacking in sound financial sense seem out of place.

The story, "The Woman Who Lost Her Beauty," told earlier (p. 13), shows an honest mistake by a well-meaning but suspicious husband. His wife, reacting to his unexplained neglect and disdain, became ill and suffered in silence, unaware of any misdeed on her part. When the truth came out, the wife was restored to everyone's good graces.

The man is presented as a proud, good husband who wrongly suspected his wife of infidelity. The wife is seen as a good, moral, uncomplaining woman, suffering quietly while loyal to her husband despite his unexplained hurtful behavior toward her.

With a different interpretation, both spouses can be seen in a less favorable light. The man becomes foolish (making rash judgments on flimsy evidence), callous (paying no attention to his wife's ill health and misery), and irresponsible (not verifying his suspicions). The woman, instead of praised for her forbearance and patience, can be faulted for not trying to learn the reason for her husband's actions, for not being assertive in her own behalf, and for not looking out for her own welfare. As the story is written, however, the woman suffers badly for her husband's mistake, and both are praised in the end for their culturally acceptable behavior. Such lack of communication between marriage partners, lack of trust and consideration on the part of a husband, and lack of self-esteem on the part of a wife are as harmful today as they have been in marriages in the past.

Currently, many published stories show a predominance of arrogant, often brutal men who rely more on physical strength and cultural prescriptions than on wisdom, kindness, or caring in dealing with their wives. And their wives tend to choose docility, underhandedness, or belligerence in dealing with these difficult marriage partners.

Appropriating stories to a reverse perspective and equalizing the roles of the spouses requires a new mind set. This outlook would include a single rather than a double ethical standard for spousal behaviors. Stories would then project a forward-looking atmosphere appropriate to today's cultural concerns over gender equality and marriage stability.

7
Wives and Husbands, Equal People

Marriage in folkstory texts is not idyllic. Happiness is greatly sought, but highly elusive. Patriarchal gender relationships are the models held up to us in most current collections despite modern rhetoric about gender equality and changing marriage norms.

At the same time, pressures for change are rising. The largescale participation of women in the work force, the cultural expectation for both spouses to provide ever greater material benefits for the family, and the increasing burden on women to fulfill both home and job responsibilities demand new outlooks. Stories of the subservient or manipulative wife, of unchallenged violence against women, and of male domestic domination run counter to these trends.

New approaches are not reflected in most folkstory collections. Traditional stories supporting hierarchic male rule and a subservient role for the wife tend to be passively accepted by today's reading public.

No other group—ethnic, racial or religious—is presented in the same light. Currently published stories do not justify subjugation of and violence against any other group of people.

Instead, public recognition of fair, non-discriminatory treatment has influenced storytelling in some areas. As has been mentioned, Zipes[1] chronicled the use of folktales in Nazi Germany to spread the poison of the 1930s by bolstering anti-semitic attitudes and glorifying the German "hero." Following the end of World War II, such stories and interpretations were fiercely discredited and efforts made to reinstate democratic, non-discriminatory themes. In the United States, a furor broke out over the racist content of the children's book, *Little Black Sambo*. This book has all but dropped from sight and from use in children's education. Ethnic jokes have become a source of embarrassment and recrimination, and no longer enjoy the popular acceptance that had been accorded to such fads as Polish Jokes a few decades ago. In general, stories urging subordination of and violence against ethnic, racial, or religious minorities are not found in current collections.

Trickster stories in which the weak, the downtrodden, and the disenfranchised challenge and overcome strong authority figures have long been a source of pleasure throughout the world. The peasant outwitting the landowner, the commoner manipulating the king, the weakling controlling the bully, the impoverished hoodwinking the miserly, these and many other such themes make us rejoice at the triumph of decency, equality, and justice. All the downtrodden overcome, except the woman as wife. Here, in the relations of wife and husband, we find the weak, the less powerful, the financially impoverished, the politically disenfranchised—the women—not only losing in the battle for moral justice, but forcibly being subjugated and demeaned.

Why the outrageous difference between men's relation to other men and men's relation to women? The question goes to the heart of feminist concerns, and addresses the enormous lack of fairness and equity in the marriage relationship.

In several recent works, scholars have grappled with this critical aspect of life. Demie Kurz[2] has written that the very structure of wife/husband roles in contemporary marriage institutionalizes control of women by men. Greer Fox[3] stresses the durability of male and female traditional roles despite more liberal mate selection practices. Based on a study of marriage in Turkey, she finds that behavior patterns of wives and husbands after marriage conform to traditional standards, whether the marriage was based on love or on parental arrangement. This view has been reinforced recently in the United States by Hochschild and Machung.[4] Studying families in the San Francisco area, they find that despite several decades of the feminist revolution, traditional family roles and behaviors have changed little. While opportunities for women have expanded greatly in outside gainful employment, expectations of female domestic responsibility and male dominance continue in the home.

These findings are mirrored in the present study of folkstory marriage. Love is rarely a factor in marriage stories. And the small number of roles available to folktale wives and husbands attests to the similarity of patriarchal marriage requirements in stories from different times and places.

How can we explain the acceptance of traditional spouse roles in life and in stories despite the modern insistence on women's liberation? Recent assessment of the results of the Women's Rights Movement can provide some insights.

Many believe that the initial goals of the Women's Movement of the 1960's have been accomplished. The struggle was to open educational and work opportunities to women, and according to Carol Gilligan, "Those changes have been made, and they really are extraordinary."[5]

Some feminist writers now are concerned with what is called the second stage.[6] The major issues are: the ideological support of women who choose to remain at home in the roles of wife and mother; and assistance to relieve women's double burden of career and home responsibilities. Current efforts concentrate on public policy issues, such as abortion rights, quality day care, and leave for family caretaking.

Important as these issues are, they do not address the fundamental status imbalance between spouses. The need for equality between wives and husbands has not yet been raised to a rallying cry.

Furthermore, as long as there remains tacit acceptance of unequal traditional domestic roles, efforts at eradicating wife abuse are likely to be unsuccessful. Although there is growing recognition of the widespread dangers of domestic violence to women, this issue has received scant political action.

Perhaps a third stage in women's activism is needed, that of finally addressing the most basic evidence of gender inequality, the relationship between husbands and wives. In this third stage, the message of the folkstories can be of value.

People seriously interested in moving toward egalitarian relationships can recognize in the traditional marriages of the folkstories, the legacy of limitations placed on spouse behavior: the distortion of the communication process, the combative postures, the need to win rather than to care, and the men's resort to physical violence—all consequences of status imbalance. The most unwholesome aspects of the marriage relationship—male dominance and physical violence—are shown to have created strife and distorted personalities from ancient times to the present.

Several scholars have pointed to striking similarities between folkstory messages and those contained in the modern media.

Television, films, magazine articles, cartoons, soap operas, and adver-
tising all borrow from and reinforce the views of the folkstories.
    Mildred Pollner states,

> Over the years, television and other media have been guilty
> of portraying married men as incompetent husbands
> [Tolerant Men] . . . either fools [Puppets] or temperamental
> tyrants [Bosses] . . . Wives are often portrayed as control-
> ling bosses [Shrews] or mothering martyrs [Good
> Women].[7]

In regard to the movies, Pollner calls attention to "the film's central drama of men, dominance and violence."[8]
    Linda Degh studied the career choices of women, by comparing
old folktales and modern media presentations. She concluded, "The
career script of women in [folk]tales . . . kept its appeal as a charter for
feminine behavior in the modern . . . era.[9]"
    That charter is:

> . . . be average . . . earn room and board in exchange for
> around the clock service in the house of a domineering hus-
> band . . . The assumption of power is the gratification of the
> hero. The heroine is his property. . .[10]

She comes to that conclusion in spite of the changes brought
about by the Women's Rights Movement of the 1960s.

> When . . . I chose to compare the narrative elements of the
> female career as designed in folktales, fairy tales and mod-
> ern magazine stories, I came to a conclusion I did not expect
> . . . the old values did not change significantly.[11]

Concerned with the contradiction of increased equality outside
the home and the persistence of traditional inequality inside the home,
students of family life have been looking for ways to bring the two into
better balance. Citing suggestions from a number of contemporary
social scientists, Demie Kurz[12] summarizes areas of greatly needed
information about modern marriage. She suggests empirical research on
the following: What are the strategies of control and power in marriage?
How different are the strategies used by women and by men? What
norms and practices of family relationships promote conflict and con-

done violence? How do women and men respond to the use of violence in marriage? What can we learn cross-culturally about male dominance and the use of violence?

As seen in earlier chapters, folktales help answer these important questions. Shrews, Wise Women and Bosses illustrate different strategies of control and power. Stories reveal bases for conflict and violence. Good Women and Shrews who turn into Good Women exhibit different responses to the use of violence. Cross-culturally, stories illustrate the almost worldwide acceptance of male dominance in marriage. Stories can help scholars respond to the call for greater understanding of marital difficulties and act as guides for further research into the traditional nature of modern marriage.

The findings presented in this book suggest that new models are needed for modern marriage. In looking to the future, we would do well to note the behavior of folkstory Assertive Wives and Husbands; they illustrate relationships appropriate for tomorrow's world.

The following behaviors, illustrated in stories of Assertive Spouses, fit with the possiblity of gender equality: pursuing mutually satisfactory solutions instead of winning; communicating openly to promote understanding; cooperating instead of maintaining silence, deception, and harshness; exhibiting respect and caring in place of a male dominated hierarchy; and rewarding peaceable settlement of domestic quarrels in place of hostility and physical abuse.

Strong public concern can produce changes in the current unchallenged acceptance of stories disdainful of women. When sufficiently forceful objections are heard, folkstories reflecting the concept of equality in marriage can replace the present models of hierarchy and violence. Disrespect and debasement need to disappear as acceptable models for today's readers and tomorrow's marriage partners.

The search for safer, happier marriages, while difficult, is clearly worth the effort. Carolyn Heilbrun urges moving away from the male dominated past toward a future for women and men "full of risk, and variety, and discovery; in short, human."[13] We ask, along with Madonna Kolbenschlag, "Can we walk out of the fairy tale into the future together?"[14]

End Notes

Notes to Chapter 1

1. For a detailed discussion, see John Nicholson, *Men and Women: How Different Are They?* (NY: Oxford UP, 1984).

2. In Peter D. Kramer, *Listening to Prozac* (NY: Viking, 1992), various case studies are presented illustrating the harmful effects of distorted perceptions in gender interactions.

3. For a more detailed discussion, see David E. Tresemer, "Assumptions about Gender Role," *Women in a Man Made World*, eds. Nona Glasser and Helen Y. Waehrer (Chicago: Rand Mc Nally 1977) 114-127. More recently, in a newspaper article entitled "Behavior that can wreck a marriage" (*The News and Observer*, Raleigh, NC 5 Dec 1993: 8E), Alison Bass wrote that research on marriage tends to be anecdotal and often contradictory.

4. Erich Fromm, *The Art of Loving* (NY: Harper, 1956).

5. This book is limited to the relationship between married partners. By extension, however, the findings can apply to cohabiting couples whose commitment to each other may be similar to legal marriage. Children as a factor in marital problems, while clearly important, is a subject outside the scope of the book. Interestingly, folkstories about spouse relationships rarely include children as part of the story. Barbara W. Tuchman also attests to the comparative absence of children in medieval literature and documentary evidence. (See *A Distant Mirror: The Calamitous Fourteenth Century.* NY: Knopf, 1978. Chapter 3). One can only speculate on the reason for these omissions.

Notes to Chapter 2

1. Carolyn G. Heilbrun, *Reinventing Womanhood* (New York: Norton, 1979)

2. Miriam M. Johnson, *Strong Mothers, Weak Wives: The Search for Gender Equality* (Berkeley, CA: U of California P, 1988)

3. Jane Caputi, "The Sexual Politics of Murder," *Gender and Society 3* (1989): 437-466.

4. Barbara J. Harris and Jo Ann K. McNamara, *Women and the Structure of Society: Selected Research from the 5th Berkshire Conference on the History of Women* Vassar College, 1982. (Durham, NC: Duke UP in affiliation with the Institute for Research in History, 1984)

5. Betty Friedan, *The Second Stage* (NY: Summit, 1981).

6. Gloria Steinem, *Revolution from Within: A Book of Self Esteem* (Boston: Little, Brown, 1992).

7. Arlie Hochschild and Anne Machung, *The Second Shift: Working Parents and the Revolution at Home* (NY: Viking, 1989).

8. Hope J. Leichter and William E. Mitchell, *Kinship and Casework* (NY: Russell Sage, 1967)

9. Stuart A. Queen and Robert W. Habenstein, *The Family in Various Cultures* (NY: J.B. Lippincott, 1974).

10. In Alison Bass' newspaper article, "Behavior," Markman is quoted as saying, "One of our findings from our work is that marriage distress only comes in a few forms, whereas there is a great diversity in marital happiness."

11. Stoeltje delineated three different kinds of women: the lady, the helpmate, the bad woman; and three different kinds of men: the cowboy, the cattleman-settler, the outlaw. She showed that these types were necessary adaptations to the hardships and requirements of life on the American frontier. Beverly J. Stoeltje, "A Helpmate for Man Indeed: the Image of the Frontier Woman," *Women and Folklore: Images and*

Genres, ed. Claire R.Farrar (Prospect Heights, IL: Waveland, 1986) 25-41.

12. For a detailed discussion of this formulation, see Lenora Ucko, "Unequal Partners: Women in Folkstory Marriage," *Mount Olive Review* 7 (1993-94): 64-73.

13. Mildred Pollner, "Better Dead than Wed," *Social Policy* 13 (1982): 28-31.

14. For example in such titles as "A Wise Wife," "A Taming of the Shrew," and "The Value of a Good Wife."

15. Two examples may suffice. Zipes describes folktales published by the Brothers Grimm as "a male dominated discourse that has had social and ideological ramifications for the civilizing process in the West." Jack Zipes, *Fairy Tales and the Art of Subversion*, (NY: Wildman Press, 1988): 23

Lundell sees popular folktale editions as promoting "a narrow view of women aimed to fit ideals promoted by nineteenth century patriarchal sensibilities." Torborg Lundell, "Gender-Related Biases in the Type and Motif Indexes of Aarne and Thompson," *Fairy Tales and Society: Illusion, Allusion, and Paradigm*, ed. Ruth B. Bottigheimer (Philadelphia, PA: U of Pennsylvania P, 1986): 149.

16. Claire Farrer recognizes that in the past men cultivated myths of female servility, which were then accepted by both men and women. These male influences continue to be reproduced in currently published folktale collections, and are perpetuated in the minds of new generations of readers. See Claire R. Farrer, *Women and Folklore* (Austin: U of Texas, 1975) for a more extended discussion.

17. For a discussion of family violence and its causes, see Murray A. Straus, R. J. Gellis, and S. K. Steinmetz, *Behind Closed Doors: Violence in the American Family* (Beverly Hills: Sage, 1981); also Murray A. Straus, *Physical Violence in American Families: Risk Factors and Adaptations to Violence in 8,145 Families* (New Brunswick, NJ: Transactions, 1990).

18. A good discussion of current difficulties in domestic relationships can be found in John Scanzoni and Maximiliane Szinovacz,

Family Decision Making: A Developmental Sex Role Model (Beverly Hills: Sage, 1980).

19. Myrna M. Weissman, "Depression," *Psychotherapy: An Assessment of Research and Practice*, ed. Annette M. Brodsky and R.T. Hare-Mustin (NY: Guilford, 1980) 97-112.

20. Deborah Tannen, *You Just Don't Understand: Women and Men in Conversation* (NY: William Morrow, 1990).

21. Caputi "Sexual Politics."

22. Heilbrun *Womanhood.*

23. Madonna Kolbenschlag, *Kiss Sleeping Beauty Good-by: Breaking the Spell of Feminine Myths and Models* (Garden City: Doubleday, 1979).

24. Ethel Johnston Phelps, introduction, *Tatterhood and Other Tales* (NY: Feminist, 1978).

25. Andrew Morton, *Diana: Her True Story* (NY: Simon and Schuster, 1992).

26. Johnson *Strong Mothers.*

27. *The American College Dictionary* (NY: Random House, 1968) 1208.

28. Johnson *Strong Mothers.*

29. An example of the destruction of a Good Woman is the fate of Desdemona in Shakespeare's *Othello.*

30. Lawrence W. Levine, *Black Culture and Black Consciousness: Afro-American Folk Thought from Slavery to Freedom* (NY: Oxford UP, 1977) 123.

31. Evelyn C. White, *Chain, Chain, Change: For Black Women Dealing with Physical and Emotional Abuse* (Seattle, WA: Seal, 1985).

32. The word *assertive* is used to describe people who are able to express their own feelings and ideas without aggressing against

another. The interaction between Assertive Spouses includes respecting each other despite differences of opinion and resolving conflicts without the need to win control over the other.

33. Stinnett, Nick and John De Frain, *Secrets of Strong Families* (Boston: Little Brown, 1985).

Notes to Chapter 3

1. Mary Ryan, *Womanhood in America: From Colonial Times to the Present* (NY: New Viewpoints, 1979).

2. William Goode, *World Revolution and Family Patterns* (NY: Free Press, 1963).

3. Johnson 231.

4. Fromm 87.

5. Note comments by Indries Shah, *World Folktales* (NY: Harcourt, Brace, Janovitch: 1979) 124, and Ewan Mac Coll, *Folk Songs and Ballads of Scotland* (NY: Oak) 37.

6. A good exposition can be found in Gerald R. Leslie, *The Family in Social Context* (NY: Oxford U P, 1982).

7. This story deals with essentially the same problem as the story,"The Woman Who Was Too Curious," told in an earlier chapter. The two stories end very differently because the spouses adhere to different cultural requirements in their marriage roles.

Notes to Chapter 4

1. Pauline B. Bart, ed., Introduction, *Gender and Society* 3 (1989): 431-436.

2. Domestic violence is the most common crime in America today, affecting 3 to 4 million women each year. Battering is the single major cause of injury to women, exceeding rape, mugging, and auto accidents combined.

3. For a more extended discussion, see Lenora G. Ucko, "Who's Afraid of the Big Bad Wolf? Confronting Wife Abuse Through Folkstories," *Social Work* 36 (1991): 414-419.

4. Demie Kurz, "Social Science Perspectives on Wife Abuse: Current Debates and Future Directions," *Gender and Society* 3 (1989): 495.

5. Bart 435.

6. See discussion in *Coalition Quarterly* (Durham/Orange County Coalition for Battered Women, 1986): 2.

7. Straus, Gellis, and Steinmetz, 42.

8. Quoted in Roberta L. Hall et al., *Male-Female Differences: A Bio-Cultural Perspective* (NY: Praeger, 1985) 138.

9. Anne Fausto-Sterling, *Myths of Gender: Biological Theories about Women and Men* (NY: Basic, 1985) 217.

10. Ann Landers, advice column, Raleigh, NC *News and Observer* (4 Sep 1989).

11. Leslie Z. Mcarthur, and Karen Apatow, "Impressions of Baby-Faced Adults," *Social Cognition* 2 (1983-84). 315-342.

12. Deborah Richardson, et al., "Male Violence Toward Females: Victim and Aggressor Variables," *Journal of Psychology* 119 (1985): 129-135.

13. Straus *Physical Violence.*

14. Marija Gimbutas, *The Early Civilization of Europe* (Monograph for Indo-European Studies 131. U of California at LA, 1980).

15. Wendy Jackson, "Can Individual Differences in History of Dominance Explain the Development of Linear Dominance Hierarchies?" *Ethnology* 79 (1988): 71-77.

16. Caputi 453.

Notes to Chapter 5

1. Leslie 273.

2. Thomas F. Thiselton-Dyer, *Folk-lore of Women as illustrated by Legendary and Traditional Tales, Folk-Rhymes, Proverbial Sayings, Superstitions* (Chicago: C.McClurg, 1906) passim.

3. Fromm 4-5.

4. William Goode, "The Theoretical Importance of Love," *Selected Stories in Marriage and the Family*, eds. Robert F. Winch and Louis W. Goodman. NY: Holt, Rinehart and Winston (1968): 470.

5. Quoted in Joyce Brothers, "How Women Love?" *Parade* (9 April 1989): 4-7.

6. Brothers 4-7.

7. Peter C. Pineo, "Disenchantment in the Later Years of Marriage," *Marriage and Family Living* 23 (1961)

8. Fromm *Loving*.

9. Niklas Luhmann, *Love as Passion: The Codification of Intimacy* (Cambridge, MA: Harvard UP, 1986).

10. Luhmann 151.

11. John Scanzoni, and Maximiliane Szinovacz, *Family Decision Making: A Developmental Sex Role Model* (Beverly Hills: Sage, 1980) 15.

12. The catastrophic effect of teaching children male domination and female subservience to patriarchal authority, whether by direct instruction or by models of parental behavior, has been explored in recent studies. This subject lies outside the scope of the present study, but the reader is referred to Elizabeth Debold, et al, *Mother-Daughter Revolution: From Betrayal to Power* (Reading, MA: Addison-Wesley,

1993); Rose Glickman, *Daughters of Feminists* (NY: St. Martins, 1993); and Victoria Secunda, *Women and their Fathers: The Sexual and Romantic Impact of the First Man in your Life* (NY: Delacorte, 1992).

13. Heilbrun *Womanhood* 196.

14. Johnson 12-13.

15. Harris and McNamara VIII

16. Tikva Freymer-Kensky, *In the Wake of the Goddesses* (NY: Free Press, 1992) 140.

17. Steinem 257.

18. Dana Vannoy-Hiller, and William W. Philliber, *Equal Partners: Successful Women in Marriage* (Newbury Park, CA: Sage, 1989) 128-129.

19. Steinem 276.

20. Vannoy-Hiller and Philliber 83.

21. Steinem 227.

22. Stinnett and De Frain *passim.*

Notes to Chapter 6

1. Brunvand, for example, referred to the "many similar elements of plot and theme occurring repeatedly in the collected folk traditions of widespread nations and different periods." Jan Harold Brunvand, *Folklore: A Study and Research Guide* (NY: St. Martin's, 1976) 10.

2. For a detailed account of cultural similarities and differences in marriage relationships, see Queen and Habenstein.

3. Brunvand states, "There are no 'correct' or 'original texts'. [and] one cannot hope to pin down the *right* text." Brunvand 4.

4. According to Dundes, even folk toys made in different countries reveal unique cultural qualities. Alan Dundes, *Folklore Matters* (Knoxville, TN: U of Tennessee P, 1989).

5. Bonnie S. Anderson, and Judith P. Zinsser, *A History of Their Own: Women in Europe from Prehistory to the Present* vol.1 (NY: Harper, 1988) xv, xvii.

6. Anderson and Zinsser 338.

7. Helen Mayer Hacker, "Gender Roles from a Cross-cultural Perspective," *Gender and Sex in Society*," ed. Lucile Duberman (NY: Praeger, 1975) 185-215.

8. Robin Morgan, *Sisterhood is Global* (Garden City, NY: Anchor,1984) 679.

9. Anderson and Zinsser 149-150.

10. Morgan 95.

11. Anderson and Zinsser xvii.

12. Delia Davin, "The Women's Movement in the People's Republic of China: A Survey," *Women Cross-culturally*, ed. Ruby Rohrlich-Leavitt. The Hague: Mouton (1975): 457-469.

13. Niara Sudarkasa, "Interpreting the African Heritage in Afro-American Family Organization," *Black Families*, ed. Harriette Pipes McAdoo (Beverly Hills, CA: Sage, 1981) 44.

14. Kamene Okonjo, "The Role of Women in the Development of Culture in Nigeria," Rohrlich-Leavitt. 31-40.

15. Paul Bohannan, *Africa and Africans* (Garden City, NY: Natural History, 1964) 164.

16. David Levinson, *Family Violence in Cross-cultural Perspective* (Newbury Park, CA: Sage, 1989).

17. Note the similarity to the African story, "The Woman Who Was a Lioness." In both stories, an animal becomes a human being to save her own kind from harm. The husbands are somewhat different. In the African story, the townspeople, not the husband, kill the wife to save the community. The brutality is much more extensive in the African American story—the hunter decimates the herd, which was not a danger, and mutilates and tortures his changed wife.

18. Lawrence W. Levine, *Black Culture and Black Consciousness: Afro-American Folk Thought from Slavery to Freedom* (NY: Oxford UP, 1977).

19. Jesse Bernard, *Marriage and Family Among Negroes* (Englewood Cliffs, NJ: Prentice-Hall, 1966).

20. Herbert G. Gutman, *The Black Family in Slavery and Freedom* (NY: Pantheon. 1975).

21. For a more detailed discussion, see Lenora G. Ucko, "Culture and Violence: The Interaction of Africa and America," *Sex Roles* 31 (1994): 185-204.

22. Raphael Patai, *Tents of Jacob* (Englewood Cliffs, NJ: Prentice-Hall, 1971).

23. Lucy Dawidowicz, *The Jewish Presence: Essays in Identity and History* (NY: Holt, Rinehart, Winston, 1977).

24. *Memoirs of Glueckel of Hameln* (NY:Shocken. 1977).

25. For a more detailed discussion, see Lenora G. Ucko, "Who Are the Wives? Who Are the Husbands?: Marriage Roles in Jewish Classical Folktales," *Jewish Folklore and Ethnology Review* 12 (1990): 5-10.

26. This situation is not to be confused with stories that retain their foreign identification and cultural attributes when retold as belonging to another culture.

27. William Bascom, "Four Functions of Folklore," *Journal of American Folklore* 67 (1954): 333-349.

28. Zipes *Fairy Tales* 7.

29. Two such collections are: Ethel Johnston Phelps, *Tatterhood and Other Tales* (NY: Feminist, 1978), and *The Maid of the North: Feminist Folk Tales from Around the World* (NY: Henry Holt, 1981).

30. Joan N. Radner, and Susan S. Lanser, "The Feminist Voice: Strategies of Coding in Folklore and Literature," *Journal of American Folklore 100* (1987): 412-425.

Notes to Chapter 7

1. Zipes *Fairy Tales.*

2. Demie Kurz, "Social Science Perspectives on Wife Abuse: Current Debates and Future Directions," *Gender and Society* 3 (1989): 489-505.

3. Greer Litton Fox, "Love match and arranged marriage in a modernizing nation: mate selection in Ankara, Turkey" *Journal of Marriage and the Family* 37 (1975): 180-193.

4. Hochschild and Machung *Second Shift.*

5. Carol Gilligan quote, Claudia Willis, "Onward, Women!" *Time Magazine* (4 Dec 1989) 82.

6. See Betty Friedan's exposition in *The Second Stage* (NY: Summit, 1981).

7. Pollner 29-30.

8. Pollner 29-30.

9. Linda Degh, "Beauty, Wealth and Power: Career Choices for Women in Folktales, Fairytales and Modern Media," *Fabula: Journal of Folktale Studies* 30 (1989): 50.

10. Degh 52-53.

11. Degh 61.

12. Kurz "Perspectives."

13. Heilbrun *Reinventing*

14. Kolbenschlag 215.

References

Abrahams, Roger D. Introduction. *African Folktales*. NY: Pantheon, 1983. xiii-xviii.

Anderson, Bonnie S., and Judith P. Zinsser. *A History of Their Own: Women in Europe from Prehistory to the Present*. Vol.1. NY: Harper, 1988. 2 vols.

Austin, Algernon, and Beth Paul. "What Makes a Marriage Work? Using Videotape to Analyze Couple Interaction." *Radcliffe News* (Summer 1991):10.

Bart, Pauline B. Introduction. *Gender and Society* 3 (1989): 431-436.

Bascom, William. "Four Functions of Folklore." *Journal of American Folklore* 67 (1954): 333-349.

Bernard, Jesse. 1966. *Marriage and Family Among Negroes*. Englewood Cliffs, NJ: Prentice-Hall, 1966.

Berne, Eric M.D. *What Do You Say After You Say Hello? The Psychology of Human Destiny*. NY: Grove, 1972.

Bettelheim, Bruno. *The Uses of Enchantment: The Meaning and Importance of Fairytales*. NY: Knopf, 1976.

Bohannan, Paul. *Africa and Africans*. Garden City, NY: Natural History, 1964.

Brothers, Joyce. "How Women Love?" *Parade* 9 April 1989: 4-7.

Brunvand, Jan Harold. *Folklore: A Study and Research Guide*. NY: St. Martin's, 1976.

Caputi, Jane. "The Sexual Politics of Murder." *Gender and Society* 3 (1989): 437-466.

Centennial Index to the Journal of American Folklore 1988-89. 101 (1989).

Coalition Quarterly. Durham, NC: Durham/Orange County Coalition for Battered Women (1986).

Davin, Delia. "The Women's Movement in the People's Republic of China: A Survey." *Women Cross-Culturally: Change and Challenge*. Ed. Ruby Rohrlich-Leavitt. The Hague: Mouton, 1975. 457-469.

Dawidowicz, Lucy. *The Jewish Presence: Essays in Identity and History*. NY: Holt, Rinehart, Winston, 1977.

Degh, Linda. "Beauty, Wealth and Power: Career Choices for Women in Folktales, Fairytales and Modern Media." *Fabula: Journal of Folktale Studies* 30.1 (1989): 43-62.

Dilorio, Judith A. "Being and Becoming Coupled: The Emergence of Female Subordination in Heterosexual Relationships." *Gender in Intimate Relationships: a Microstructural Approach*. Ed. Barbara J. Risman, and Pepper Schwartz. Belmont, CA: Wadsworth, 1988. 94-107.

Ditzion, Sidney H. *Marriage, Morals and Sex in America*. NY: Octagon, 1975.

Dundes, Alan. *Folklore Matters*. Knoxville, TN: U of Tennessee P, 1989.

Farrer, Claire R., ed. *Women and Folklore*. Austin: U of Texas P, 1975.

Fausto-Sterling, Anne. *Myths of Gender: Biological Theories about Women and Men*. NY: Basic, 1985.

Fox, Greer Litton. "Love match and arranged marriage in a modernizing nation: Mate selection in Ankara, Turkey." *Journal of Marriage and the Family* 37 (1975): 180-193.

Freymer-Kensky, Tikva. *In the Wake of the Goddesses.* NY: Free Press, 1992.

Fromm, Erich. *The Art of Loving.* NY: Harper, 1956.

Friedan, Betty. *The Second Stage.* NY: Summit, 1981.

Gilligan, Carol. Quote. *Time Magazine* 4 Dec 1989: 82.

Goode, William. *World Revolution and Family Patterns.* NY: Free Press, 1963.

___. "The Theoretical Importance of Love." *Selected Studies in Marriage and the Family.* Eds. Robert F. Winch, and Louis W. Goodman. NY: Holt, Rinehart and Winston, 1968. 468-480.

Goody, Jack. *The Development of Family and Marriage in Europe.* NY: Cambridge U, 1983.

Gutman, Herbert G. *The Black Family in Slavery and Freedom.* NY: Pantheon, 1975.

Hacker, Helen Mayer. "Gender Roles in a Cross-cultural Perspective." *Gender and Sex in Society.* Ed. Lucile Duberman. NY: Praeger, 1975. 185-215.

Hall, Roberta L. et al. *Male-Female Differences: A Bio-Cultural Perspective.* NY: Praeger, 1985.

Harris, Barbara J., and Jo Ann K. McNamara, eds. *Women and the Structure of Society.* Selected Research from the 5th Berkshire Conference on the History of Women. Vassar College, 1982. Durham, NC: Duke UP, in affiliation with the Institute for Research in History, 1984.

Heilbrun, Carolyn G. *Reinventing Womanhood.* NY: Norton, 1979.

___, *Hamlet's Mother and Other Women.* NY: Columbia UP, 1990.

Hochschild, Arlie and Anne Machung. *The Second Shift: Working Parents and the Revolution at Home.* NY: Viking, 1989.

Jackson, Wendy. "Can Individual Differences in History of Dominance Explain the Development of Linear Dominance Hierarchies?" *Ethnology* 79 (1988): 71-77.

James, E. O. *Marriage and Society.* NY: Hutchinson's U Library, 1952.

Johnson, Miriam M. *Strong Mothers, Weak Wives: The Search for Gender Equality.* Berkeley: U of California P, 1988.

Jordan, Rosan A., and Francis A. de Caro. "Women and the Study of Folklore." *Signs* 11 (Spring 1986): 500-518.

___, and Susan J. Kalcik, eds. *Women's Folklore,Women's Culture.* Publications of the American Folklore Society, no. 8. Philadelphia: U of Pennsylvania P, 1985.

Jurich, Marilyn. "She Shall Overcome: Overtures to the Trickster Heroine." *Women's Studies International Forum: Women and Folklore* 9 (1986): 273-279.

Kolbenschlag, Madonna. *Kiss Sleeping Beauty Good-by: Breaking the Spell of Feminine Myths and Models.* Garden City: Doubleday, 1979.

Kramer, Peter D. *Listening to Prozac.* NY: Viking Press, 1992.

Kurz, Demie. "Social Science Perspectives on Wife Abuse: Current Debates and Future Directions." *Gender and Society* 3 (1989): 489-505.

Lamphere, Louise. "Women and Domestic Power: Political and Economic Strategies in Domestic Groups." *Being Female: Reproduction, Power and Change.* Ed. Dana Raphael. The Hague: Mouton, 1975. 117-130.

Landers, Ann. Advice Column. Raleigh, NC *News and Observer* 4 Sep 1989.

Leichter, Hope J. and William E. Mitchell. *Kinship and Casework.* NY: Russell Sage, 1967.

Leslie, Gerald R. *The Family in Social Context.* NY: Oxford UP, 1982.

Levine, Lawrence W. *Black Culture and Black Consciousness: Afro-American Folk Thought from Slavery to Freedom.* NY: Oxford UP, 1977.

Levinson, David. *Family Violence in Cross-cultural Perspective.* Newbury Park, CA: Sage, 1989.

Luhmann, Niklas. *Love as Passion: The Codification of Intimacy.* Cambridge, MA: Harvard UP, 1986.

Lundell, Torborg. "Gender-Related Biases in the Type and Motif Indexes of Aarne and Thompson." *Fairy Tales and Society: Illusion, Allusion, and Paradigm.* Ed. Ruth B. Bottigheimer. Philadelphia, PA: U of Pennsylvania P, 1986. 149-163.

Mace, David R. *Marriage East and West.* Garden City, NY: Doubleday, 1960.

Marriage and Inequality in Chinese Society. Studies in China, 12. Berkeley: U of California P, 1991.

Mcarthur, Leslie Z., and Karen Apatow. "Impressions of Baby-Faced Adults." *Social Cognition* 2 (1983-94): 115-142.

Memoirs of Glueckel of Hameln. NY: Schocken. 1977.

Morgan, Robin. *Sisterhood is Global.* Garden City, NY: Anchor, 1984.

Morton, Andrew. *Diana: Her True Story.* NY: Simon and Schuster, 1992.

Mount, Ferdinand. *The Subversive Family: an Alternative History of Love and Marriage.* Boston: Unwin, 1983.

Nicholson, John. *Men and Women: How Different Are They?* NY: Oxford UP, 1984.

Okonjo, Kamene 1975 "The Role of Women in the Development of Culture in Nigeria." Ed. Ruby Rohrlich-Leavitt, *Women Cross-Culturally: Change and Challenge.* The Hague: Mouton, 1975. 31-40.

Patai, Raphael. *Tents of Jacob*. Englewood Cliffs, NJ: Prentice-Hall, 1971.

Phelps, Ethel Johnston. *Introduction. Tatterhood and Other Tales*. NY: Feminist, 1978.

___. The Maid of the North: *Feminist Folktales from Around the World*. NY: Henry Holt, 1981.

Pineo, Peter C. "Disenchantment in the Later Years of Marriage." *Marriage and Family Living* 23 (1961): 3-11.

Pollner, Mildred. "Better Dead than Wed." *Social Policy* 13 (1982): 28-31.

Queen, Stuart A., and Richard W. Habenstein. *The Family in Various Cultures*. NY: J.B. Lippincott, 1974.

Radner, Joan N., and Susan S. Lanser. "The Feminist Voice: Strategies of Coding in Folklore and Literature." *Journal of American Folklore* 100 (1987): 412-425.

Richardson, Deborah et al. "Male Violence Toward Females: Victim and Aggressor Variables." *Journal of Psychology* 119 (1985): 129-135.

Rohrich, Lutz. Introduction. *Fairy Tales and Society: Illusion, Allusion, and Paradigm*. By Ruth B. Bottigheimer. Philadelphia: U of Pennsylvania P, 1986. 1-12.

Rohrlich-Leavitt, Ruby, ed. *Women Cross-culturally: Change and Challenge*. The Hague: Mouton, 1975.

Rosenthal, Bernice Glatzer. "The Role and Status of Women in the Soviet Union: 1917 to the Present." Rohrlich-Leavitt.

Rubin, Lillian. *Intimate Strangers: Men and Women Together*. NY: Harper and Row, 1983.

Ryan, Mary. *Womanhood in America: From Colonial Times to the Present*. NY: New Viewpoints, 1979.

Scanzoni, John and Maximiliane Szinovacz. *Family Decision Making: A Developmental Sex Role Model.* Beverly Hills: Sage, 1980.

Shah, Indries. *World Folktales.* NY: Harcourt, Brace, Janovitch, 1979.

Spiegel, John P. "The resolution of role conflict in the family." *A Modern Introduction to the Family.* Eds. Norman W. Bell and Ezra F.Vogel. NY: Free Press, 1960. 361-381.

Steinem, Gloria. *Revolution from Within: A Book of Self-Esteem.* Boston: Little, Brown, 1992.

Stinnett, Nick and John De Frain. *Secrets of Strong Families.* Boston: Little Brown, 1985.

Stoeltje, Beverly J. "A Helpmate for Man Indeed: the Image of the Frontier Woman." *Women and Folklore: Images and Genres.* Ed. Claire R. Farrer. Prospect Heights, Ill.:Waveland Press, 1986. 25-41.

Straus, Murray A. *Physical Violence in American Families: Risk Factors and Adaptations to Violence in 8,145 Families.* New Brunswick, NJ: Transactions, 1990.

Straus, Murray A., Richard J. Gellis, and Suzanne K. Steinmetz. *Behind Closed Doors: Violence in the American Family.* Beverly Hills: Sage, 1981.

Sudarkasa, Niara. "Interpreting the African Heritage in Afro-American Family Organization." *Black Families.* Ed. Harriette Pipes McAdoo. Beverly Hills, CA: Sage, 1981. 37-53.

Taggart, James M. *Enchanted Maidens: Gender Relations in Spanish Folktales: Folktales of Courtship and Marriage.* Princeton, NJ: Princeton UP, 1990.

Tannen, Deborah. *You Just Don't Understand: Women and Men in Conversation.* NY: William Morrow, 1990.

Thiselton-Dyer, Thomas F. *Folk-lore of Women as illustrated by Legendary and Traditional Tales, Folk-Rhymes, Proverbial Sayings, Superstitions.* Chicago:C.McClurg, 1906.

Tresemer, David E. "Assumptions about Gender Role." *Women in a Man Made World*. Eds. Nona Glasser and Helen Y. Waehrer. Chicago: Rand McNally, 1977. 114-127.

Tuchman, Barbara W. *A Distant Mirror: The Calamitous Fourteenth Century*. New York: Knopf, 1978.

Ucko, Lenora G. "Culture and Violence: The Interaction of Africa and America," *Sex Roles* 31 (1994): 185-204.

___. "Unequal Partners: Women in Folkstory Marriage," *Mount Olive Review* 7 (1993-94): 64-73.

___. "Who's Afraid of the Big Bad Wolf? Confronting Wife Abuse Through Folkstories," *Social Work* 36 (1991): 414-419.

___. "Who Are the Wives? Who Are the Husbands?: Marriage Roles in Jewish Classical Folktales," J*ewish Folklore and Ethnology Review* 12 (1990) 5-10.

Vannoy-Hiller, Dana, and William W. Philliber. *Equal Partners: Successful Women in Marriage*. Newbury Park, CA: Sage, 1989.

Wallis, Claudia, "Onward, Women!" *Time Magazine* 4 Dec 1989. 80-89.

Webster, Sheila K. "Women and Folklore: Performers, Characters, Scholars," *Women's Studies International Forum: Women and Folklore* 9 (1986): 219-226.

Weigle, Marta. *Spiders and Spinsters: Women in Mythology*. Albuquerque: U of New Mexico P, 1982.

Weissman, Myrna M. "Depression," *Women and Psychotherapy: An Assessment of Research and Practice*. Eds. Annette M. Brodsky and Rachel T. Hare-Mustin. NY: Guilford, 1980. 97-112.

White, Evelyn C. *Chain, Chain, Change: For Black Women Dealing with Physical and Emotional Abuse*. Seattle, WA: Seal, 1985.

Wolfram, Sybil. *In-Laws and Out-Laws: Kinship and Marriage in England*. NY: St. Martins, 1987.

Zipes, Jack. *The Brothers Grimm: From Enchanted Forest to Modern World.* NY: Routledge, 1988.

___. *Fairy Tales and the Art of Subversion.* NY: Wildman Press, 1983.

List of Stories

Index

About the Author

Lenora Greenbaum Ucko has taught anthropology and sociology at several universities, including Adelphi University, University of Massachusetts-Boston, and Hunter College-CUNY; and in addition at Boston University and the University of Maryland in Europe. She is currently a research and human resources consultant in North Carolina and teaches part-time at Duke University. She is the author of several recent articles on gender relations in marriage and on the use of folklore in social services.

Dr. Ucko received her Ph.D. in anthropology and sociology at The Ohio State University. Among her honors are a socio-psychological research award from the American Association for the Advancement of Science and an appointment as Visiting Research Scholar at the Bunting Institute.